More praise for *Built to Love*

"The most intensive and thorough discussion I have ever seen explaining the strategies that can bring the added value of emotional pull to a product or service platform. In the automobile industry, the process of leveraging emotion has been perfected by car design over decades, and Boatwright and Cagan have formalized and condensed the essence of this successful approach into the type of 'guidebook' other industries have been waiting for."
—Chris Bangle, former Chief Designer, BMW and Partner and Managing Director, Chris Bangle Associates, SRL

"By providing not only functional but emotional value, good product design can build brand loyalty and increase profit margins. With its analytical approach and fresh case studies, *Built to Love* demonstrates how even the most utilitarian business-to-business products can appeal to buyers' emotions—and offers practical tools any business can use to enhance product value. It's must-reading for anyone interested in understanding why today's aesthetic imperative reaches well beyond traditional fashion businesses."
—Virginia Postrel, author of *The Substance of Style*

"In good economic times and bad, businesses must seek ways to avoid the commoditization of their products and services. Peter Boatwright and Jonathan Cagan, through their analysis of supported and associated emotions, provide a road map by which we can identify and validate emotion-based opportunities and develop product and program solutions that will delight our customers now and in the future."
—William Lambert, CEO, Mine Safety Appliances Company (MSA)

"As Peter Boatwright and Jonathan Cagan point out, 'emotion is human and its reach is vast.' Technologists tend to ignore the power of emotion in their designs and products, in part because they respect reason and distrust emotion, but also because engineering tools have not addressed the emotional side of design. *Built to Love* combines lessons from marketing, emotion theory, psychological measurement, and engineering design to provide tools for designers and engineers so that their products can properly engage the emotions. Now there can be no excuse for not acting."
—Don Norman, Breed Professor of Design, Northwestern University, and author of *Emotional Design*

Built to Love

Built to Love

Creating Products That Captivate Customers

Peter Boatwright & Jonathan Cagan

Berrett–Koehler Publishers, Inc.
San Francisco
a BK Business book

Berrett-Koehler Publishers, Inc.
235 Montgomery Street, Suite 650
San Francisco, CA 94104-2916
Tel: (415) 288-0260 Fax: (415) 362-2512 www.bkconnection.com

Ordering Information
Quantity sales. Special discounts are available on quantity purchases by corporations, associations, and others. For details, contact the "Special Sales Department" at the Berrett-Koehler address above.

Individual sales. Berrett-Koehler publications are available through most bookstores. They can also be ordered directly from Berrett-Koehler: Tel: (800) 929-2929; Fax: (802) 864-7626; www.bkconnection.com

Orders for college textbook/course adoption use. Please contact Berrett-Koehler: Tel: (800) 929-2929; Fax: (802) 864-7626.

Orders by U.S. trade bookstores and wholesalers. Please contact Ingram Publisher Services, Tel: (800) 509-4887; Fax: (800) 838-1149; E-mail: customer.service@ingrampublisherservices. com; or visit www.ingrampublisherservices.com/Ordering for details about electronic ordering.

Berrett-Koehler and the BK logo are registered trademarks of Berrett-Koehler Publishers, Inc.

Printed in the United States of America

Berrett-Koehler books are printed on long-lasting acid-free paper. When it is available, we choose paper that has been manufactured by environmentally responsible processes. These may include using trees grown in sustainable forests, incorporating recycled paper, minimizing chlorine in bleaching, or recycling the energy produced at the paper mill.

Library of Congress Cataloging-in-Publication Data

Boatwright, Peter.
   Built to love : creating products that captivate customers / Peter Boatwright & Jonathan Cagan.
      p. cm.
   Includes bibliographical references and index.
   ISBN 978-1-60509-698-8 (alk. paper)
   1. New products. 2. Product management. 3. Customer relations--Management. I. Cagan, Jonathan, 1961- II. Title.
   HF5415.153.B625 2010
   658.5'75--dc22   2010024210

First Edition
15 14 13 12 11 10   10 9 8 7 6 5 4 3 2 1

Interior design and project management by Jonathan Peck, Dovetail Publishing Services
Cover design by Irene Morris

Built to Love is dedicated to people we particularly love:

Kerri, Annabel, Brayden, and Elliana

Leslie, Melissa, Joshua, and Ben

Contents

Foreword

Donna J. Sturgess
President, Buyology Inc,
formerly Global Head of Innovation, GlaxoSmithKline

For most of my professional career, marketers have worked to create value in products by developing rational features and benefits, like new or faster functionality. The fundamental weakness with this approach is that, as consumers, our responses to rational features account for only 15 percent of all the decisions we make. The rest of the decision process operates subconsciously, where emotion dominates. The result of the traditional marketing approach is that customers experience a "sense" gap.

It is time for business to come to its senses and recognize that emotion is the single greatest lever it has in accelerating market performance. Emotions are how customers derive meaning and value in any product that we use. Authors Peter Boatwright and Jonathan Cagan argue that it is emotional content that drives product awareness, stimulates word-of-mouth, and motivates repurchase. When a company leverages emotion, the company benefits before the customer purchases the product, during the customers' use of the product, and after the consumers' product experience ends and they seek a new one.

This doesn't happen by luck. Product emotions must be designed. Companies must intentionally design the emotion-based experience that customers desire into the core of their business, leading to products that evoke a positive emotional response by exceeding expectations on important benefit dimensions. Emotion results in an increase in customer attention, persuasion, and memory retention. The more touchpoints the consumer experiences in a product or service, the greater the level of interaction, emotional engagement, and impact on their long-term memory of the product. When robust rational and emotional strategies synchronize, the resulting momentum thrusts the business forward, resulting in the acceleration of market performance.

Since you picked up this book, you no doubt recognize there is something missing in business strategies today. As you read the insightful research and examples the authors provide, I offer you four keys to consider: First, emotion matters in every type of business; next, more sensory interaction in the customer experience is better than less; and third, emotion has to be managed strategically.

Built to Love proves that emotion pays off, and it presents an approach to break emotion into attributes that provide the basis for an emotion-based strategy. Toward the end, the book extends to a wide range of disciplines that gives you a grand finale fireworks display of emotion and its value within the context of any business. Oh yes, and the fourth key that you will realize from this book is that emotion results in increased profit!

So what are you waiting for?

Preface

This is a book about emotion. *Built to Love* celebrates the value that customers get from using products that make them feel great, so great that they begin telling everyone about those products. When designing new products, companies often work really hard to make new products *work better* than existing ones, missing the opportunity to provide products that make customers *feel better*. For those companies that do address customer emotions, most do not address emotions through the product itself. Rather, they set their hopes on marketing campaigns, seeking to generate excitement about the product regardless of whether the product will deliver on the promise. This book reveals a different approach, one that provides products that authentically generate emotions customers will value so much that the market lights up with intense interest in and passion for the product.

Built to Love is written for those of you who are executives, who set the vision and direction for your firm, to give you the insights you need to bring out new products that energize your customers. It is also written for marketing managers and product managers, who are responsible for fulfilling customers' needs and wants, to show you how to increase your market share by satisfying a broader and more vital set of customer desires. Further, we address professionals in the world of product development and design, to help you bring out products that engage customers to the extent that they demand your product and only yours. We also wrote the book for the rest of you who are not in the product development world, but who want to understand how the products you love are developed.

We focus not just on physical products but also on services, software, and brands. We discuss both consumer products and business-to-business products, from large companies and those as small as startups.

Conversations with industry leaders highlighted the need to prove that valued emotions lead to product success, to provide metrics to support your company's investment in an emotion-based product development process, and to provide a methodology for integrating emotion as a basis for product strategy. This book provides that proof and process.

Built to Love is a result of our research into new product development methods, our experience in consulting with firms to strategize and design new products, and our experience in teaching product development methods and new product marketing.

We celebrate the balance between functional performance and emotional reward, providing clear evidence that emotion pays off. Our scientific studies demonstrate that successfully delivered "product emotions" will result in better company performance and higher perceived value by customers.

To move the theory into practice, we provide a how-to guide for uncovering the emotions that should drive the development of a new product. We also provide insight into how such a product emotion strategy will result in products that people love.

Chapters 1 through 5 begin with *why*: why product emotion is real, why it is critical to all types of products, and why it is profitable to leverage when developing products in good economic times or bad. We include statistical proof of emotion's value by examining stock performance of high-emotion companies and how high-emotion features impact the value of individual products. For readers who practice product development, this first part will equip you with arguments that show how product emotions are critical to your future product development efforts.

After showing that authentic emotion really does pay off, we move on to *how* in Chapters 6 through 10: how emotion can be broken down into its core building blocks, how it is then used to develop new products, and how product touchpoints—in particular visual touchpoints—deliver those emotions. These chapters go on to show how to translate emotions into a strategy to develop products that stimulate emotion in customers, create a buzz about brands, and create a group of passionate and loyal customers. For the practitioners, this second part will present a process to follow in order to design product emotions.

Throughout the book, engaging case studies from a variety of industries will help you understand how to integrate emotion into your products and brands, regardless of the nature of your business.

We have a passion for great products. We appreciate the effort that companies take to make our experience in using their products engaging, pleasurable, and satisfying. Our goal in this book is to help others understand why such emotions are not due to luck but are the result of strategic and skillful product design. Our goal is to help all companies create products that are built to love.

Built to Love

Energizing the Marketplace

In today's marketplace, there is a new kind of leading company. These leaders do not just produce good products. They produce captivating products that energize the marketplace and set the standard for what customers want and expect. To see if your firm is one of these new leading companies, think about your firm's best product. Are customers excited by it, not just purchasing and using it, but also talking about it? Is there a hum in the marketplace about your product, where your product is the topic of media discussions and social media posts? If so, your company is one of today's new leaders.

If, however, people find your product useful but not captivating, acceptable only because there is no better alternative, then there is no marketplace electricity; there is no love. Your product may provide the best performance or latest technology, but people lack enthusiasm. If they buy your product, it is out of necessity or unthinking habit. If this scenario describes your firm, then your customers would welcome some alternative to excite them, something to pull them out from the humdrum of ordinary good products. *The difference between an ordinary product and a captivating product is emotion.* When emotion flows in the marketplace, your product shines. When there is no emotion from the product, customers lack the enthusiasm and passion that launches a product to success.

For those of you who love using a particular product or service, you know the sheer pleasure you get from using it. You are aware that there are competing products that are similar in technology and performance, and others may wonder where your passion comes from. You know the enjoyment you derive from the product is real, that you are not a mindless victim of some marketing ploy. It is the product itself that captivates you, both by its performance and by how it actually makes you feel.

Seeing the impact and influence of the products from today's leading firms, can others achieve similar results? More specifically, can your firm deliberately design products to be captivating? After extensive research, we have found that answer to be a clear "yes." The answer lies in designing product emotions, namely, emotions evoked by the product itself.

People, your customers, have emotional desires as well as the need to perform tasks. Many firms know they need to stimulate emotions, but they attempt to create them artificially. Some companies will paint a misleading picture of their products, describing emotions that people don't really feel when using the product. This short-term attempt to trick the customer into buying a product will fail in the long term, resulting in customer dissatisfaction and frustration.

We believe that the product itself must be designed *from the start* to evoke emotions that resonate deeply with the customer, resulting in passion in the marketplace and customer commitment to the company.

In short, the product must be built to love.

Built to Love

This is a book about emotion, about what customers desire from products as well as why certain products and companies successfully captivate the marketplace. We celebrate the joy that comes from owning, working with, or using exciting products.

This is also an analytical book, with studies to validate our insights, providing proof that emotion is the source of captivating, and profitable, products. Building on these insights, *Built to Love* is a practical book that shows how your company can create high-emotion, highly valued products. In sum, this book provides an argument and a how-to guide for how to make emotion flow from your product—from the ground up.

Emotion is fundamental to all that is human, including the products that we enjoy. Emotion fuels the satisfaction people feel when using a product and strengthens their desire to repurchase that product. It is emotion that instigates people to tell others about the products they own; indeed, word-of-mouth is the most powerful marketing force in today's networked marketplace.

You may be presuming that only certain products can stimulate emotions, consumer products such as fashion clothing and iPods, and not products like industrial gas lines, engineering software, robotic tools for manufacturing, and business services. We will show you that emotion-based opportunities exist for all products, from consumer to business-to-business products, from luxury goods to everyday commodities.

We found that product emotions are relevant to all kinds of physical products as well as to services, software, processes, and brands. All of these various kinds of products deliver emotions and are opportunities for emotion-driven profit, so we use the word "product" in the inclusive sense. The tools, methods, and arguments throughout *Built to Love* apply to the whole array of products. By analyzing examples of many types of products, this book formally and analytically demonstrates why emotion is such an important part of new product development, revealing how any company, small or large, can create innovations that customers must have.

You may believe that most companies are already using emotional appeals to stimulate purchase of whatever they are selling, whether cars or computers, tools or telephones. There is a difference between manipulating emotions to sell a product versus providing a product with emotional benefits that a customer truly values. *Built to Love* is not about emotional manipulation. It is about providing real value to customers by creating products that authentically provide emotional benefits.

Supported versus Associated Emotions

To evoke emotions such as confidence, safety, joy, pride, and other feelings, a firm may follow one of two paths, as shown in Figure I.1. One path is that of "supported emotions," evoked by the product itself; we also refer to these as "product emotions." For example, a sense of excitement, adventure, power, and passion are all supported by a well-designed sports car. To be highly valued by customers—to be *built to love*—supported emotions must be deliberately designed into the product. In the sports car, these emotions come from more than acceleration; they are also delivered through an aggressive vehicle stance, a loud muffler, and low-sitting minimalist seats that allow the car to look fast and the driver to feel the road.

The excitement of product emotions is not only found in sporty vehicles but can be built into *any* product, physical or otherwise, including consumer electronics, flexible pipe used for connecting natural gas lines, toys, nonprofit services, and many others, all explored in this book.

The second path is that of "associated emotions." These are not evoked by the product itself but are superficially created through repeated associations with emotions distinct from the product. A tobacco company, for example, may suggest that its cigarettes will make consumers feel more masculine and self-confident. The cigarettes themselves do not create these feelings, but the company designs strong masculine images on billboards and in advertising to convince consumers to associate these cigarettes with feelings of power.

Unlike supported emotions, which are fulfilled by the product, associated emotions may be manipulative, unfulfilled claims intended to profit the firm

FIGURE I.1 ■ A Model of the Paths to Emotion. Supported emotions result in products built to love.

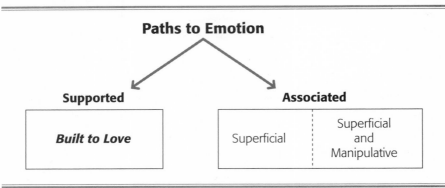

while possibly harming the consumer. With tobacco companies, the result of using the product is not increased masculine strength for the smoker, but potentially debilitating weakness (or worse, death) from cancer.

Associated emotions are not all manipulative. Some may merely exaggerate the supported emotions or provide fantasies to consumers in a way that is superficial but honest and open (like a frog that sings the name of a beer). Nonetheless, without supported emotions there can be no long-term satisfaction. There can be no love.

The first part of this book (Chapters 1–5) digs deeply into these classes of emotions and examines how high-emotion features impact the overall value of individual products through supported emotions. This is shown in products ranging from long-haul trucks to electric vehicles to the packaging of your iPod. We first explain the context of product emotion then scientifically analyze its profitability. One aspect of analysis is at the macro level of the firm. We introduce a stock index for high-emotion companies (as determined by consumers). Our analysis of historical returns shows that high-emotion companies outperform standard indices, even through a down economy. This first part of the book shows that emotion pays off.

Creating Products that Captivate Customers

Dell, HP, and Lenovo deliver cutting-edge technology at a good price. But these companies and their products are not clearly differentiated from each other. Apple stands out from the pack by delivering emotional experiences to a

FIGURE I.2 ■ Creating products that captivate customers.

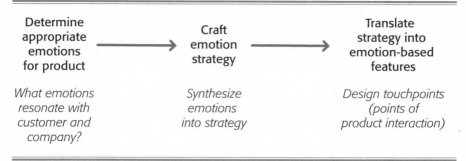

loyal customer base. As a result, their products—both physical and services—earn serious profit margins. Why aren't more companies like Apple? Why don't more companies offer not just products that get things done, but product emotions as well? Our answer is that most companies don't understand that Apple (and Google and many other high-emotion firms) derive their success from emotion, by delivering products built to love.

The second part of the book (Chapters 6–10) introduces a method to identify relevant emotions for a given market, a way to specifically target those emotions, and a means to craft them into a strategy that drives future product development, as shown in Figure I.2. What's most exciting is that we will introduce you to an actionable tool that will guide you through this process. We then show how to create emotional touchpoints, points of interaction between the product (or company) and the customer. Touchpoints are the means to deliver emotions to the customer. Case studies from the extremes of social action to raw technology drive home the benefits and depth of product emotions.

A Book Written for You

We are university professors who teach and research innovation, and we have developed a scientific basis for product emotion. As consultants to a wide variety of large and small business-to-business and consumer companies, we have applied our insights in technology, durable goods, transportation, packaged goods, medical devices, utility and software products, services, and brands. We have advised over 200 innovation teams and successfully guided companies in the development of high-emotion commercial products and product portfolio strategies.

Built to Love is a product of our experience. We have written this book because we have seen a vast and accessible opportunity for firms, an opportunity that many firms consistently overlook. Although products are designed to create value for their customers, and although people value emotions, firms often overlook how they can provide emotional value to their customers.

With this in mind, we have written *Built to Love* to be a practical guide to how companies can develop a strategy to create products that fulfill human value in the broadest sense. We show how to fulfill the needs and desires that people are seeking through the products they buy and use.

There may be several reasons why you are reading this book:

- You may be responsible for the success of products in your firm. You get it: You understand the importance of product emotions, but those under you don't. It's just not the way they were trained. Or maybe those above you don't get it, and you have found it frustrating when you have tried to justify your insights to those who don't understand but make the decisions. Until now you have had no metrics or statistics to prove your point. This book will provide you with logical arguments and statistical proof that product emotion pays off. It will teach why and how. You can use this book to show others how Apple or Google, for example, continue to maintain such strong brands and customer loyalty. *Built to Love* will provide lots of examples of how emotion can be a truly powerful and lucrative force in your industry.

    One important lesson is that success does not require creative genius (or luck). *Built to Love* provides a formal methodology that your company can follow to integrate emotion into your products.

- Perhaps you have heard that there is substance to the idea of product emotion, and you are curious to find out more. You might be a marketer who has always thought that emotion is generated alongside but not from a finished product, as a way to get initial sales going. You might be an engineer or technologist who has yet to see how this kind of extra effort or "fluff" will make your cutting-edge technology any better. *Built to Love* provides proof that product emotion is real and that it can be lucrative if sincerely and authentically integrated into your products and brands.

- You might be searching for a method to engender emotions for your products in your customers. You are seeking a means to integrate emotion into your product development process. *Built to Love* provides a method to develop an emotion-based strategy and to deliver that strategy in a cost-effective way.

■ It may be that you are just intrigued by the concept. Maybe you saw this book while walking through a bookstore or airport, or you heard about it from a friend. You might not be involved at all in the development of products but just interested in the idea of product emotion, or intrigued by how emotions can be designed, or wondering why you love your iPhone (or some other product) so much that you use it happily every day. We hope you will enjoy the discussions and case studies as we give you a peek at how products electrify the market.

We are going to journey through the marketplace of emotions, a journey that we ourselves have taken to write this book and have found to be intensely exciting. This isn't a mere thrill ride; it's a scientific journey into a world where products are built to love.

CHAPTER 1

Product Emotions

We have all seen large "big-rig" trucks rambling down the interstate. Each of those 40,000-pound vehicles is a small business on wheels, driven by an employee or by the business owner himself. For trucks, as with other small businesses, business profits require efficiency. Fuel-cost increases have made profit margins slimmer than ever before, and weight restrictions (on the whole truck—cab and trailer) mean that every pound counts. Money is made delivering payload, so the weight in the cab is minimal, maximizing payload weight.

The truck is not only a business, but is also a home—a very small home, roughly the floor area of a two-person tent, a mini room in which the driver needs to sleep, eat, and change clothes, and also watch movies, read, play video games, and do deskwork. There is no separate living and sleeping area, no place to change or freshen up, few places to store belongings, and no place to prepare even a sandwich. This is where the driver spends his time while on the road.

The more that goes into that home to make the driver's life better, the more it both costs and weighs, reducing business efficiency. Long-haul truck interiors have therefore been designed as efficient, lightweight spaces with minimal creature comforts, allowing drivers just enough space for sleep so they can get back on the road. Even for those U.S. drivers who own their vehicle and sacrifice some fuel economy for the classic look of an American truck, the vehicle interior remains sparse.

What had been overlooked, or not recognized as important, was the opportunity to design the truck interior to be more than an efficient business tool. The drivers consider themselves professionals, making sacrifices to be away from family and friends. The life of a trucker can be tedious, lonely, and uncomfortable. Employee turnover is greater than 100 percent per year among fleet drivers, which means that drivers' lifestyle needs are significant to the industry.

In 2008, Navistar's International Truck, a longstanding brand that had become known only as a basic workhorse, introduced LoneStar, a different kind of long-haul truck. New management at Navistar recognized the underlying dual needs of those in the trucking profession: the need to keep costs low with efficient business tools along with the need to transform a monotonous and stressful task into a more comfortable and enjoyable profession. Navistar understood that the trucker longs for family and friends, needs a place to unwind, wants a good night's sleep, and requires simple, convenient meals. Navistar realized that truck drivers lacked positive emotional experiences on the road. LoneStar answers the duality of truck industry needs, for LoneStar is a paradigm-shifting truck that fulfills emotional desires while also delivering superior performance.

LoneStar is a bold, classic-looking truck, with styling features that hark back to the 1930s and '40s, while clearly setting a styling trend for the 21st century. Truckers love chrome and LoneStar uses chrome elegantly and plentifully on the exterior, with chrome just about everywhere chrome can be. Its bold, pronounced grille gives the truck command of the road, and pride in the ride.

On the inside, unlike traditional trucks with cramped, spartan living spaces, LoneStar's interior is more like a cabin in a private jet. Its interior incorporates amenities that have not been available in standard trucks: features for cooking, eating, sleeping, and relaxing. Unlike other trucks with two bunks, there is a full-sized bed in LoneStar; it folds up Murphy-style, revealing a crescent-shaped couch. A kitchenette with food storage, microwave, and refrigerator allows for simple meal preparation, and a pullout table provides space to eat and work. Airline-like overhead storage keeps the cabin neat and organized. Hardwood flooring, a television, and a seven-speaker Monsoon sound system complete the living experience.

The interior design and its features make the driver feel professional, successful, and comfortable, all in a roughly 4-by-7.5-foot space. At the same time that the truck is specifically designed for the trucker's emotional and lifestyle desires, business needs such as fuel economy were taken seriously. At its introduction, LoneStar was arguably the most fuel-efficient long-haul vehicle on the planet, the most aerodynamic for headwinds and winds from any direction, because winds do come from all directions.

It may be no surprise that Navistar had plenty of pre-orders on the truck. The surprise is that truck drivers also stood in line at the truck's introduction to have the LoneStar logo permanently tattooed to their arm (in some cases both arms) without yet owning or even having driven the vehicle. That's a truck that was built to love! LoneStar is much more than a great truck. A functional truck designed to offer emotional opportunities like no other, LoneStar is also a means to re-invigorate and reposition Navistar's entire brand.

FIGURE 1.1 ■ Interior (birds-eye view from above) and exterior of innovative LoneStar long-haul truck by Navistar's International Truck brand.

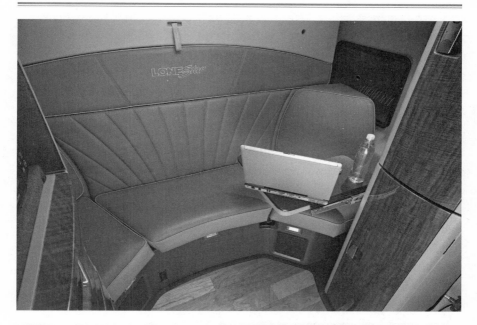

Photos courtesy of Navistar

Obviously, most companies would want their products to rouse customers as successfully as LoneStar has. Rather than creating products that themselves captivate customers, many companies attempt to build interest through loyalty programs, catchy campaigns, or other add-on programs. Odd as it may seem, it is quite common to attempt to engage customers by doing anything but changing the product itself!

This is what Navistar used to do. Formerly, their strategy was to make functional, cost-effective products. Engineers made the product for its functions rather than to serve emotional needs; when trying to sell it, the sales group used emotional appeals, hoping to interest customers. Instead of competing for the top-loved brand, they competed for the lowest-margin commodity. This is the way many companies have long treated emotion, as something to evoke after the product is built in order to make the sale. This is a fundamentally different approach from meeting an emotion-based opportunity head-on.

Today Navistar makes its trucks both for functional purposes and to fulfill emotional ones. Driving a truck from Cleveland to Kansas City, a driver delivers the goods to the destination. Driving a LoneStar also allows the trucker to enjoy the pleasure of getting there. If the truck did not get the goods from Cleveland to Kansas City, nobody would be satisfied, no matter how exciting the truck is, not the trucker nor their client. The result would be negative emotions such as anger, loss, neglect, or incapability.

Meeting functional needs is a requirement to prevent negative emotions, but success goes far beyond preventing negative emotions. People love a product not only because it serves their task, but because it serves emotions related to their task as well. For the trucker, just getting from Cleveland to Kansas City is not enough. The trucker prefers to get there in a way that makes him or her feel proud, powerful, comfortable, professional, and successful. There is more to the experience than the functional task; the lifestyle benefits of the experience are important as well.

Navistar aggressively and consistently used an emotion strategy to drive development of LoneStar. Throughout *Built to Love* we revisit Navistar's transformation from being commodity driven to emotion driven, uncovering customer-desired emotions and translating those into a product emotion strategy. In Chapter 7, we demonstrate how that strategy produced a series of exciting new trucks, including LoneStar, partly through a high-emotion, visual form language.

Navistar is one of many case studies explored in *Built to Love*. Not all companies understand that emotions cannot be an add-on, an afterthought, and still engage their customers. Emotions that powerfully engage customers are those that are core to the very reasons to make the product in the first place: because it will be a product that customers value. A product built to love.

Product Emotions Everywhere

To recognize the relevance of emotion in products other than trucks, let's ask a basic question: Why do people buy things? It is an essential question to business, a basic concept that may seem simple to answer. Yet many companies do not truly understand why customers are willing to spend extra for one product when it accomplishes the same tasks as a cheaper alternative. Why are customers fanatically loyal to one product yet indifferent to another?

So why *do* people buy things? Customers purchase products both for *what the product does* for them, namely, "product functions," and also for *how the product makes them feel*, what we call "product emotions." Consider cars, for example. People require transportation. One function of cars is to provide the ability to move us from place to place. Customers also buy and use cars to fulfill emotional desires in addition to functional needs. Some want to feel well taken care of, so they especially enjoy luxury cars replete with comfort features such as leather seats, high-end audio, and cup holders that keep their morning coffee warm. Some want to feel "green" with a car that reduces the carbon footprint, even at added cost. These non-functional attributes create emotional value in the vehicle, fulfilling emotional wants. People buy products that make them feel better or safer or prouder.

Consider an example of a smaller product that you might use every day. When the iPhone came out in 2007, other products such as the Palm Treo already met all of the core functional deliverables of the iPhone. But the iPhone, with its ease of use, sexy interface, and beautiful aesthetic, led people to feel empowered, joyful, and well cared for. The iPhone also overcame the significant impediment of being relegated to a single service provider. Consumers have been amazingly willing to leave their existing service providers to become iPhone users.

The iPhone initially succeeded not because of its functionality but because of its product emotions: the emotions people felt when they saw, touched, and used the product, and the way they integrated it into their lives and lifestyles. The result was love. One iPhone owner recently told us, "It's not perfect, but I love it." Similar phrases of love are echoed in various ways among iPhone customers and by Apple customers in general.

A Product Only for Emotion

Possibly the ultimate "how it makes me feel" product is music. There is no functional need fulfilled by music; music is all about emotion. Music makes you feel happy or melancholy, energetic or restful. Music can connect you to memories and experiences. Remember the school dance when you first heard "Free Bird," or the time on the beach listening to Bob Marley, or the Bach minuet they played at your wedding? The desire to hear music and feel those emotions results in an industry valued in tens of billions of dollars.

The emotion of music is integral to many experiences such as movies, where the suspense, happiness, and romance are foretold and amplified through music. How menacing would Darth Vader be without the deep repetitive horns in minor key announcing Vader's presence? Close your eyes when you listen, and you feel Vader even without seeing him. Or how exciting would Indiana Jones' escape-from-certain-death be without the contrasting upbeat, energetic, and frenetic iconic tune in major key? The musical pieces for these two movies were written by the same composer, John Williams, who clearly understands how to use music to create, mold, and direct a range of emotions.

Emotion and the Senses

Any product that elicits an emotional response must reach a customer through one or more of the five senses. To experience a product is to touch, use, see, feel, or taste it. Every time we touch, use, see, feel, or taste the product, we react to that experience with emotion, feel something inside that makes us enjoy or resent or desire or abhor the experience. Products that are not perceived by any of the senses will not directly convey emotion. For example, engine parts will have a purely functional role if they are never touched or seen or smelled or heard by a person, even though the engine as a whole produces a hum and vibration that excites the driver.

Any product with which a person interacts has the potential to deliver emotion. With music, the sense of hearing is all that is needed to capture the core product emotion. Yet emotions, positive or negative, can be amplified when delivered to more senses, such as adding a visual element to the music. Classic album artwork is, at times, revered to the level of the music itself. Music videos, which combine the visual and the auditory, are today core to the music industry. The encounter with sound, art, and motion work in concert, providing at its best a heightened emotional experience through a perfect blend of the senses.

FIGURE 1.2A ■ Webkinz stuffed animals (well-loved collection of Ben and
Joshua Cagan).

Photo by Melissa Cagan

Or take a simple stuffed animal, which reaches customers through its visual appearance and quality of touch. Both elements, the appearance and the feel, can be manipulated in sync to achieve emotional goals. The fur of an aggressive-looking stuffed tiger might feel bristly, while the fur of a cuddly-looking tiger feels soft.

Beyond visual appearance and physical sensation, how can a company that makes toys give a turbo-boost to the simple stuffed animal, already the ultimate emotional connection for young children? Toy manufacturers have found ways to add technology to stuffed animals, connecting with more senses. Tickle-Me-Elmos that talk and vibrate remained popular for a decade, with hordes of people standing in line for holiday purchases.

And yet, as much as the extra technology in Elmo offers the surprise and joy for the first weeks or months, few children carry that Elmo or any other tech-laden toy with them through every night, every car ride, every visit to the store, every doctor's office for comfort, as they do with their favorite, simple stuffed animal. How can a company create a more ongoing stream of emotions for the traditional stuffed animal?

FIGURE 1.2B ■ Screenshots from webkinz.com, which depict the virtual version of the physical stuffed animals in their room, and provide games for kids to play.

In 2005, Ganz, a Canadian company headquartered in Woodbridge, Ontario, added a whole new dimension of sensory experience to stuffed animals, merging the ultimate "lovie" with the ultimate game forum to create Webkinz. Webkinz are soft, adorable, stuffed animals—cuddly koalas, plush pugs, cute kittens—that can be loved and dragged around like any other stuffed animal. Open the tag on its collar and go on the Internet to www.webkinz.com, type in a code, and a virtual version of the animal appears. A child sets up a user name that associates with the code, names their animal, and they can spend hours upon hours playing games (some educational), looking for gems, cooking, buying virtual clothes and toys for their pet with virtual dollars they earn playing games, and tending for the well-being of their pet.

Within two years and without advertising, over a million Webkinz users were registered. In what had been a declining industry, Webkinz sales have continued to grow steeply, reaching a broad range of children, most of whom have more than one Webkinz pet. Webkinz are a somewhat new craze, but unlike Cabbage Patch dolls and other crazes that are static, Webkinz have a dynamic element that expands the interactive pleasure of the stuffed animal experience with the exploration of new games, accessories, and actions, in addition to the basic stuffed animal that itself connects emotionally to the children.

All Ganz needs to do to keep kids coming back for more is to update activities on its website. Kids connect to Webkinz in a deep and emotional way, expressing joy, love, enthusiasm and more, and the cost margin for Ganz is minimal, producing low-cost physical toys and creating, maintaining, and updating a website.

Emotions and the Web

The web world is filled with all kinds of products that provide services and also connect emotionally with customers. Amazon and eBay satisfy the desire for non-invasive shopping for anything and everything you might want, with the ability to window-shop from the comfort of your home. With its maps, Google offers the adventure of exploration by providing directions in the physical world, and Google Maps echoes the experience with enjoyable exploration of the software itself: street views, user images, Wikipedia data, data overlays, and more.

Facebook and YouTube facilitate emotion by connecting people to one another and encouraging us to talk about whatever we want to talk about, typically issues or items about which we feel strongly (again, emotion). All of these products connect to our lives via the capabilities that the products enable, and how much they mean to all the individuals who use them, and have feelings about them.

Examples Abound

Think of other emotion-laden products that stand out. KitchenAid's Pro Line toasters, waffle makers, coffee makers, and contemporary-styled dishwashers integrate into the kitchen environment, creating a professional-styled kitchen that projects one's love of and skill for food. BMW cars excite customers and project speed, luxury, and wealth, while Honda cars promote confidence, social responsibility, and practicality. Harley and Indian Motorcycles connote freedom, Americana, and fun. Because these products fulfill both the emotional yearning of consumers as well as utilitarian function, they generate significant margins.

Once you begin to see the value of product emotions, examples abound. Emotion is core to any consumer or business relationship. The fact that customers seek to fulfill both functional needs ("what it does for me") and emotional desires ("how it makes me feel") is true for every physical or virtual product, service, or strategy—a computer, a hospital visit, express package delivery, a kitchen blender, a vacation cruise.

It is also true for business products. When one thinks of business-to-business (B-to-B) products, one usually thinks about capability—the functionality that is required or enabled. It may not seem like emotion really matters for products found in utilitarian functional environments. Upcoming chapters will demonstrate the importance of product emotions such as trust, security, and empowerment in multiple B-to-B companies, because it turns out that whenever people are involved, emotion matters. Regardless of context, customers buy products for both what the product does for them and how the product makes them feel. There is great opportunity for business-based products to deliberately evoke emotion, to be built not just to perform but also be built to love.

Product Emotions versus Emotional Decisions

Many firms recognize that emotions matter, but they attempt to *use* emotions rather than *provide* emotions. Such firms attempt to get the consumer into an emotional state of mind, where the consumer makes an emotional decision to buy the product. This use (or misuse) of emotions is often what people think of when they say that marketers attempt to sell them what they don't need.

People's decisions are certainly affected by their emotions. Someone who is sad has been shown to be willing to spend more money on products than those who are not sad, because sadness causes people to want to change their circumstances.[1]

Our emotions can also be altered by our surroundings. Music influences our emotions and the energetic or sedate style of background music in advertising has been shown to affect our perceptions of products at purchase.[2]

Many decisions naturally involve emotion. A parent who is planning a family vacation to Disney World may feel anxiety over travel arrangements and financial costs, emotions surrounding the decision of whether to take the vacation. The emotions of the decision are generally quite different from those felt while using and experiencing the product. That parent will feel entirely different emotions while at Disney World, experiencing the joys of family fun and making memories that linger.

Emotional decisions are entirely different from emotions evoked by the product. The decision is in the past but the consequences remain for the long-term future. A frugal consumer may be delighted with the bargain she struck when replacing her car, but years later her emotions about the car will be less about the initial transaction and more about her experience with the vehicle.

Product emotions are ongoing, substantiated, and renewed with each product experience. Product emotions have the power to completely replace the range of emotions that surrounded the original purchase decision. Unlike emotions meant to provoke a quick sale—here today and gone tomorrow—product emotions are designed to endure for the lifetime of product use.

Let Your Customers Do the Talking

When products create valued emotions that endure over the life of the product, customers benefit. Companies that provide those well-loved products also benefit. The product that exudes an ongoing stream of positive emotions promotes a "feel-good" aspect, reinforcing customer satisfaction with the purchase, setting up for repeat purchases, and increasing the likelihood of receiving the best (and cheapest) form of advertising: word-of-mouth.

Emotion is what causes people to talk about products. Maybe the consumer feels surprised by how well a new technology works and tells a colleague. Maybe a consumer feels proud of their car and shows it off to clients. Maybe a consumer relishes the feeling of the pampering of a spa and asks friends to join her. Emotion leads to word-of-mouth, whose power is authenticity and an exponential expansion to more potential buyers.

On the flip side, when consumers are not emotional about a product, they don't talk about it. That means no word-of-mouth, no sales expansion beyond those who initially tried it out. Even worse, negative emotions can lead to word-of-mouth in a detrimental way, as resentful customers naturally complain to their friends. Emotion gets people talking, and positive product emotion is critical for new product success.

Product emotions are more powerful now than ever before, because there has been a fundamental shift in how the marketplace operates. We now live in a globally networked society, where consumers learn more about products from each other on the Internet than they do from direct-to-consumer advertising. As traditional advertising channels have less and less power and as individual consumers have increasing influence, product emotions have become even more critical to product success.

Product Emotions and Product Strategy

Certainly, a product should include more than just emotional value. The performance attributes of the product must deliver value for customer satisfaction in the short-term and long-term. The feeling of quality ties to actual quality, the feeling of safety ties to actual safety, and in vehicles, the feeling of control ties to the actual control.

In the 1990s Chrysler had significant quality problems with their transmissions. Cars with thoughtful lifestyle features (and surprises like hooks to hold grocery bags, to the delight of customers at the grocery store) and aggressive styling soon disappointed customers as their transmissions failed, sometimes right after their warranties ran out. These surprises did not delight and, as a company, Chrysler lost customers for the long-term.

In this case, the quality that was originally tied to the emotions of satisfaction, security, contentment, and honor led to customer emotions of uncertainty, envy, lack of consideration, and vulnerability. It's not just the vehicle with the faulty transmission that loses equity, but the Chrysler brand as a whole. Although multiple factors contributed to the downturn in the U.S. auto industry at the early part of the 21st century, lingering emotions like these could not have helped.

Companies must have a long-term strategy for product emotion and a process to deliver high-emotion products. When a company designs or produces a product, emotions will be intentionally or unintentionally infused into the product as the customer experiences that product. A company can and must intentionally design an emotion-based experience, meaning that the company's product should evoke emotions that their customers desire to experience over the life of the product and not simply to stimulate purchase. These ongoing emotions are the means to enable a brand and set of products to resonate with its customers, fueling the firm's growth and profits.

Conversely, companies who are unintentional in planning for emotions leave it to chance. In order to intentionally deliver high-emotion experiences, a company must understand why emotion is important and identify those emotions that matter to its customers. These emotions will form the basis for a product emotion strategy from which products are designed. Accomplishing this is not arbitrary. A rigorous process of innovation is required to consistently understand which emotions are desired and to evoke those emotions in products while also fulfilling needs.

Product emotions must be designed; products must be built to love!

The Emotion of Brands

Customers associate emotions with the product and also with the brand. A large part of the value of a brand is nothing more than emotion, the remainder of that value coming from information that the brand conveys about the company or product. For many people, a brand is a signal of quality, where even the basic trademark is thought to indicate the quality of the company that it represents. That quality signal certainly leads to an emotional benefit of the feeling of security and trust in that company's products.

The brand, however, is more than a signal of quality, providing intangibles such as passion, excitement, and an honest relationship between the company and customer. For example, the fact that the Chrome browser (a product) comes from Google (a brand) is informative about product quality. Because it is a Google product, users expect it to safely install on their local machines without fear of a Trojan horse virus. The value of the Google brand goes even beyond the assurance that it can be safely installed. Customers feel a sense of satisfaction and empowerment when using any high-performance product that Google provides. Google's mission is to "organize the world's information and make it universally accessible and useful." Google's brand message is an optimistic one: the dream that anything is possible. Optimism is emotional; optimism and hope are valued in addition to the utility value of the product.

Put differently, consider that there are many browsers for personal computers, and Google's Chrome browser offers its current functionality as well as the promise and excitement of future developments. The ultimate goal is to create emotions supported by the product and associated with a brand. The product must deliver appropriate emotions to build equity in the brand and, although intangible, the brand must consistently communicate appropriate emotions to create desire for the product.

Emotion in Lean Economic Times

When the economy is prosperous, people have money readily available to spend on emotion. When the economy is poor, customers are clearly careful about how they spend their money. Companies feel pressure to focus on cutting costs. It may seem that in lean times product emotions therefore become less important. In downturns, however, product emotions become even more critical to companies. When spending carefully, customers need additional incentive to buy, and seek greater value for the money. Product emotions are generally an efficient way to provide that value.

Which emotions are valued most can shift during lean times. Rather than pampering or bling or extravagance, customers may seek reassurance through comfort, stability, and attentiveness. Ironically, they often will pay additional margins to achieve these reassuring feelings even in economically lean times, because even when resources are scarce, customers are not seeking the cheapest product, but the best value.

Product emotions often play a hidden role in buying decisions, as customers may rationalize purchases on the basis of functional benefits, even though the underlying appeal may be emotional. A young lawyer may join a prestigious country club because of the thrill of being a member of that echelon (an emotional benefit), and she will justify the expense by reminding herself of the potential for meeting future clients there (a functional benefit). The iPhone user might appreciate the sleek design, fun apps, and the ability to surf the web while waiting in the car (feeling connected and contemporary), yet he rationalizes the purchase by telling everyone (including himself) about his ability to answer email while on the road.

Especially in lean economic times, companies must provide true functional benefits that provide long-term or future value. Yet providing tangible functional value isn't enough to make the sale. Without the exclusivity of the club, the lawyer would not consider joining. If the iPhone did not provide emotional fulfillment, most consumers would not purchase it, regardless of its functionality. Without emotion, these purchases might never even happen.

Product emotions provide essential benefits even in lean economic times. Are they worth the extra costs to the producer? From a company's viewpoint, costs are a major concern in downturns, as production expenses may become more constrained than during periods when sales are higher. Producing product emotions does not have to cost significant money, because emotions may be created through more careful attention to already existing features of the product.

In software, careful attention to usability (such as clear wording for menus), interaction (such as fewer clicks per task), and aesthetics (such as a contemporary and professional appearance) can greatly enhance a user's experience yet cost little more to achieve. Similarly for physical products, attention to ergonomic details or styling need not cost any more to produce. Such benefits are valued by customers and cost little to realize, which can significantly boost profit margins.

From the company viewpoint, product emotions have the benefit of helping a firm's product to stand out among competitors. If several products are available to meet functional needs, then the customer will focus on other characteristics of the product to select among the many. Appropriate emotion provides that differentiation. The result will be a hot product that meets both functional and deep emotional needs. To quote Eric Schmidt, CEO of Google, "Innovation has nothing to do with downturns. A hot product will sell just as well in a recession as it will in a nonrecession."[3] A hot product is an emotional product. Google is one of many companies that understand emotion. Their customers have passion for the capabilities that Google gives them. If your customers are not passionate you haven't reached a sufficient level of emotion.

The Transformation

Product emotions are valued everywhere, yet the opportunity to leverage product emotions is so large in part because so few firms have focused on them as a primary purpose of their products. Think again about our opening discussion of the LoneStar long-haul truck. When considered merely as a tool of business, trucks should be designed to maximize output (miles) while minimizing costs (no frills, no added weight). Because trucks have always been viewed that way, most trucks are cost-driven, minimalist products. But when a company recognizes an emotion-based opportunity and considers lifestyle support for the driver, using this particular truck can become an emotional experience for the user. With proper execution the resulting product will be revolutionary, like LoneStar.

The story of long-haul trucks is the story of most products in the U.S. during the latter part of the 20th century. Emotion-based opportunities were not the goal. Most products were designed primarily or even exclusively for the functions that they performed. Efforts were focused on achieving higher-quality performance of those functions while holding costs in check. For many companies, the drive to reduce costs often neglected the experience of using the product, sacrificing high-margin product emotions for tight-margin minimalism. LoneStar, and the many other case studies discussed in this book, serve to demonstrate that products can and should be designed to fulfill emotion-based opportunities. Product emotions are critical to long-term business success.

Understanding the value of product emotions will not simply transform a company's tactics and marketing but change its product strategy and perhaps even its mission. For companies accustomed to creating customer value through the performance of their products, the goal is to build on that foundation of performance while adding product emotions. People buy and pay for what they value, and everyone values emotion.

Creating valued emotions is not coincidence or luck, nor need it be the result of creative genius. Anticipating and meeting emotional needs requires rigorous analysis, a method that helps the company to identify desired emotions, to understand those emotions, and then to translate that understanding into a strategy for brand development, for product and portfolio development, and for specific product features.

Built to Love is about that method, a rigorous and analytical approach to identify and understand emotions and to translate that understanding into company profits. First, let's understand the benefits of emotion, so that designing them is clearly worth the effort.

CHAPTER 2

Profitability of Emotions

It all gets back to money at some point, and the question of whether or not it is profitable for your firm to provide product emotions. A cost-benefit analysis is a relatively straightforward task for how a product functions. Take, for example, a technology that would increase fuel efficiency of existing cars, adding three extra miles of travel for each gallon of gasoline. That efficiency translates into real money for drivers. Extra fuel efficiency can be valued by how much drivers save in dollars. Firms can then trade off the driver's fuel-cost savings with the cost of manufacturing and delivering that fuel-efficient technology. If the amount that drivers save dramatically exceeds the cost of providing it to them, it's a no-brainer. If how much money drivers will save is a pittance relative to the cost, again the decision is simple. If it is close, the manufacturer has a decision to make, but at least it is an informed one based on real dollars.

How does one go about a cost-benefit analysis for product emotions? Just how valuable are they? Company leaders may recognize that product emotions are potentially profitable, but they also know that every opportunity has its costs. Many designers know in their gut the power and the potential benefits of product emotions, but they don't know how to show their upper management that the resulting products will pay off in the end. Still others believe that emotion-based design is a black art, that only luck will give you a truly high-emotion product, and they don't know how to justify putting resources in areas where there appears to be no guarantee of success.

This chapter discusses revenues and costs. After presenting product emotion revenues in the context of well-known successful companies such as McDonald's, DeWalt, and Starbucks, we also talk about the costs. The major point about the costs of designing with product emotions in mind is that they are typically very low. In Chapters 3–5 we will provide evidence to convince any skeptics that emotion pays off—and does so handsomely. To begin here, we consider how emotion fits into basic economics. Thinking back to Econ 101, how are revenues and costs related to emotion? More pointedly, can knowledge of basic economics help us to understand how to increase consumers' value for products and simultaneously increase profitability and overall company performance?

Emotion-based Revenue

Revenues are affected by price and by sales volume. Revenues go up if the firm increases the price while maintaining at least the same sales volumes. Revenues will also go up if the firm sells greater volumes of product without lowering the product price. So it gets down to two questions: If a firm adds emotions to a product, will product sales increase enough to pay the costs of creating the emotions? If a firm can deliver emotions in a product, can it increase the product price enough to pay for the cost of creating the emotions?

At McDonald's, Customers Are Lovin' It

Let's start with the sales volume question and consider one of the most high-volume businesses in the world: McDonald's. McDonald's serves 50 million meals per day. Consider the coordination of buying, preparing, and selling so much food, on time, day after day, all over the globe. What an unbelievably efficient system! More than simply delivering food, it must be prepared correctly for geographically tailored menus and tastes, and all food consumed must be safe to eat.

Consider, as a hypothetical example, a situation where one person in a billion served could get salmonella. If even a single person got such a disease, it would be a major problem for McDonald's. Given that there are six and a half billion people in the entire world, it would seem that it would take a long time for a billion people to even be served. McDonald's serves 50 million meals per day every day, so in our hypothetical example it would only take three weeks for someone to get quite ill. In reality, they don't! The McDonald's system is superbly refined for safe delivery of an extremely high volume of meals.

In light of their amazingly high volume of meals served, it is easy to begin to think that McDonald's real business is food output. McDonald's is an operations business, coordinating global inputs, inventory, processes, and outputs. In reality, that's just one half of their business, making sure food is available to those who want it.

The other half of McDonald's business is to generate demand, which is to provide reasons for individuals to choose to stop at their restaurants rather than those of competitors. To do so, McDonald's has to provide something valuable to real individuals who are making real-time decisions. McDonald's works to provide value to two groups of consumers in particular: kids and adults-on-the-go.

Kids get to play at McDonald's. In some outlets, they may experience the challenge of climbing towers and the thrill of descending through tubular slides, and they share the excitement of other children. Children relate to Ronald, the Hamburglar, and the fantasy of visiting the home of these characters. And of course, there is the toy that comes with their Happy Meal. Even if children never touch their fries, they want to come back. By providing fun to children and not just food, McDonald's ends up not only with sales volume but also with repeat business, or "customer retention."

While children choose McDonald's for the fun, adults choose McDonald's because of its simplicity and efficiency. If an individual is hungry and needs a meal fast, isn't it so easy to pull up to the ubiquitously nearby McDonald's and quickly satisfy the need? Thinking about yourself, are you one who visits McDonald's because of the taste of the food and for how healthy it is for you? Is it because McDonald's is the best-tasting and healthiest meal for that point in time? Or, knowing that the food tastes good enough, are you someone who visits McDonald's because of its simplicity and efficiency?

Simplicity and efficiency are essential to quick-service restaurants. In addition, there is emotional value. For children, the Golden Arches lead to anticipation and fulfillment of fun, the joy of being at McDonald's. For adults, it is not only that McDonald's *is* simple and efficient, but also that McDonald's *feels* uncomplicated, *feels* efficient. There is the *feeling* of security in knowing that McDonald's is all about the efficient provision of a decent meal. When adults need a quick meal they seek out McDonald's. When they see the Golden Arches, they get a sense of relief and "problem solved," assured about its efficiency, and comfort in its simplicity.

To understand the importance of these emotions, imagine that you stop at McDonald's and it doesn't *feel* fast enough as you wait in the drive-through line. Now you are even more stressed, tapping your fingers, grumbling about anything and everything, all because the feeling isn't right. There is much that McDonald's must do to remain a fast-food leader, part of which is to provide the product emotions that lead so many people to repeatedly choose this restaurant instead of the alternatives. When aggregated from individuals to markets, this feeling yields great sales volume and high customer retention.

The Emotions of Tradesmen

Besides leading to greater sales volume and higher customer retention, emotion can lead customers to be ready and willing to pay more for the product. Think of the emotions that stem from product quality, such as the feeling of luxury, of security, confidence, pride, prestige, assuredness, and others. While it may be clear that these emotions are valued in a luxury product such as a weekend stay at a Four Seasons resort, what about something ordinary, like a tool? During use in construction or repair work, tools are sure to get beaten, scarred, dented, and dirty, so would product emotions be relevant to and valued for tools?

Consider the case of Black & Decker. Before 1991, Black & Decker's tool line had a dismal 9 percent market share among professional tradesmen. Even so, multiple product tests for their professional-grade tools found their product quality on par or better than all major competitors, even those like Makita which had 50 percent market share for the professional tradesmen segment.[4] In the arena of professional industrial users—large, commercial contractors and manufacturing assembly lines—Black & Decker was one of the leading firms. The performance level of Black and Decker's professional-grade tools was not the reason for its low market share among tradesmen.

The difference in the two professional tool segments, industrial and tradesmen, provides a clue to understanding Black & Decker's situation. Both segments have very similar tool needs. Both need reliable and durable tools, for they lose money with any downtime from tools that stop working. Considering Black & Decker's different rate of success between the two segments, one must think about the differences in how the two segments operate.

A key between tradesmen and industrial workers is the tradesman's self-reliance in getting their next job; they are not handed work orders to tell them what to do next. Tradesmen prove their own worth, and their tools are a badge of their professionalism and skill. Black & Decker tools couldn't be used as a mark of professionalism because they looked just like the same tools found in any homeowners' garage. One tradesman was quoted as saying, "On the job, people notice what you're working with. If I came out here with one of those Black & Decker gray things, I'd be laughed at."[5]

In 1991–1992, Black & Decker rebranded its professional-grade tools as DeWalt. The rebranded line was given a new look. Rather than the black and gray of the Black & Decker tool line, DeWalt tools were manufactured in a bright construction yellow. Under the Black & Decker name, the tools were already high quality but DeWalt tools were launched as a prestige brand. Similar to separate first-class check-in lines at airports, the company created separate DeWalt entrances to their existing Black & Decker service centers, where DeWalt users were provided loaners during repair if their tools broke. The rebranded tool line was massively successful. By 1994, DeWalt had 40 percent of the tradesmen segment and Makita's share was down to less than 30 percent.[6]

The DeWalt rebranding case is interesting because it so clearly separates the value of product quality from the value of product emotions. Under the brand name of Black & Decker, a brand known for popcorn poppers and Dustbusters, their tradesmen-grade tools had very low market share despite the high levels of performance and manufacturing quality. The tools had great success when sold under the new DeWalt name, because DeWalt offered professional emotional value, which supported the confidence and capability of tradesmen. Today, DeWalt is a visible leader in professional tools, priced as a premium product and commanding high sales shares, a double win for profitability.

How Much Do Emotions Cost?

What are the costs of evoking emotional responses to products? Anything extra put into products generally ends up increasing their costs. Is the cost of product emotions so high that it outweighs the gains from higher prices and sales volumes?

Cost is always an unavoidable consideration. It turns out that for product emotions the costs can be affordably low, and accessible to every firm, not only the global giants.

Product Emotions versus Advertising

Consider the product emotions of Starbucks. Starbucks products provide emotions such as tranquility, the feeling of being well cared for, and the feeling of refreshment. You may be thinking about Starbucks coffee but that is not really their product.

Starbucks has been described as "your third place," that space to relax that is neither work nor home. In founder Howard Schultz's words, "We're in the business of human connection and humanity, creating communities in a third place between home and work."[7] Starbucks provides a comfortable, relaxed atmosphere that encourages meetings and reading time. The emotions provided by Starbucks, experienced at the point of delivery, have created value that has fostered growth of the enterprise to over 15,000 stores in only 20 years. Although

Starbucks had troubled times through 2007 and 2008, Starbucks had phenomenal success up until those years and afterwards.

Throughout its earlier period of growth, Starbucks had no national advertising campaigns or the expense of national advertising, attributing their growth to word-of-mouth from those who were delighted by their product. An interesting ongoing challenge for them will be to maintain their third-place identity in addition to providing high-quality coffee, because competitors offer features that Starbucks initially withheld, such as free Internet access and readily available power outlets.

The costs of Starbucks' product emotions are low relative to the advertising expenses typically used to introduce a new product. Clearly the growth of Starbucks Corporation without the use of ad campaigns serves as further evidence of the benefits, and justification for costs, of product emotions.

Product Emotions versus Performance Features

Another way to consider the costs of emotions is to compare them to the costs of other product benefits. Going back to product quality versus quality-related emotions such as confidence and pride, typically a product's performance features and production quality require greater monetary investment to achieve than do quality-related emotions. For both physical products and non-physical products (such as services), product emotions are often evoked through visual cues, verbal statements, pointed features, and thoughtful interaction.

Prior to creating the DeWalt brand, Black & Decker could have invested to further increase tool performance or product life, except their tools were already beyond the threshold of excellent quality. Additional investment in technology to further advance quality would have been quite costly, and it was unlikely that the marginal improvement in quality would have invigorated the brand to the high level achieved by the rebranding.

Consider the cost of just one of the details of the rebranding discussed above: color. Before rebranding their tools as DeWalt, Black & Decker sold black and charcoal-gray tools in both their professional and consumer product lines. Competitors' professional tools were in highly differentiated bright colors such as red (Milwaukee), teal (Makita), and green (Hitachi). When Black & Decker rebranded their tools as DeWalt, they brought out products in bright yellow with black trim.

Product color requires a trivially small investment (especially as compared to improving product performance), yet in tools it engenders a disproportionately valued emotional response, visually conveying professionalism. The cost of a "no downtime" program was similarly low—an offer of free loaner tools if a DeWalt tool needed to be repaired. By doing so, DeWalt created the emotion of confidence in the new brand yet the program was not likely to cost much to run after it was set up; given the manufacturing quality of their tools, the loaner service would be used infrequently in practice.

Product emotions have a strong connection to specific product features. The cost of emotions is merely the cost of thoughtful execution of product functions. Confidence, contentment, and feelings of distinctiveness often stem from observable aspects of product quality, such as leather for vehicle seating, thickness of paper for stationery, or lobby décor for services such as banks or attorneys. McDonald's provides the peace of mind of simplicity and the relief of the easy, quick meal. These emotions of simplicity and the relief of anxiety would be difficult to provide were they not authentic to the actual service of McDonald's. To a great extent, McDonald's truly does consistently provide a quick meal.

McDonald's also does so much more. The menu is organized into an accessible structure and placement, the wrappers are easy to open (even one-handed), the restaurants are built in easy-access locations, and the flow through the waiting line is orderly and readily communicated. While the functional aspects of restaurant location and of the operational organization for a quick meal require a large investment, the emotional ease of simplicity is supported and communicated from details like the wrappers and packaging. Much of the infrastructure investment in simplicity can be undone if a consumer gets frustrated when attempting to open a package or if they cannot find their preferred item on the menu. While relatively inexpensive, details like packaging are essential elements for the emotional value of McDonald's. When emotions arise from the function of the product, they validate and make the actual functional attribute "real" from the point of view of the customer.

The cost of one hamburger wrapper is the same as another, yet the details of McDonald's hamburger wrappers are so important to delivering an ease-of-use experience. Conveniently, McDonald's simplicity in product packaging makes assembly in the kitchen equally beneficial, for food handlers can wrap up the burgers that much faster, increasing throughput. This is a win-win example of providing emotional benefit while reducing costs.

The cost of providing emotional value to customers are generally costs that the company would expend anyway, which means that it need not cost extra at all to provide emotions. Thoughtful color, form, and ergonomics are usually no more expensive to produce than drab, hard-to-use designs. However, it takes a certain kind of skill to think through and design emotion-based features. This might mean new skill training for a current workforce (as simple as reading this book or as time-intensive an investment as continuing education). It might mean hiring a new member of the product development staff with skills to analyze and design for emotion. It might even entail a technology-based company hiring an industrial designer.

When RedZone Robotics, a high-tech company discussed further in Chapter 6, began their growth as a renewed company (they had been in Chapter 11 bankruptcy before current CEO Eric Close bought them and successfully rejuvenated the company), the seventh employee they hired was an industrial designer, for just this reason.

It would be misleading to say that product emotions are never more costly to create. New technologies might be needed to meet a customer's emotional desire. But if it is so critical to the customer that they *must* have it, then clearly the cost will be justified by the product sales. More likely, if addressing emotion is just slightly more costly, then if a firm offers features customers don't want or features that reduce the customer's emotional connection, removing those aspects of the design readily reduces product costs, keeping overall costs in check. It may cost a little additional time to research what the customer wants, but the costs of research and planning end up being swamped by the resulting added profitability.

Infusing the product with emotion can have negligibly low costs, as low as the cost of being deliberate in designing a hamburger wrapper. In theory, it can be extremely profitable to provide emotion to customers. The theory is (1) consumers value emotion; (2) firms can provide emotion through their products—their physical products, software, services, and brand; and thus, (3) delivered emotions can be profitably offered in the marketplace.

How does theory play out in practice? In the next chapter, we analyze firm performance to see if firms that engender a positive emotional response are more profitable than firms that do not.

CHAPTER 3

The High-Emotion Index:
Stock Market Gains from Emotion

Product emotions are valued, so products that deliver them should generate additional revenue. The previous chapter concluded that the costs of providing product emotions can be quite low, implying that product emotions can be profitable. In practice, what do we find? Are firms that successfully provide product emotions more profitable than those that do not?

In this chapter we look at the macro level of the firm. In particular we want to find out if those companies that are the best at creating emotion are also the most profitable. The goal is to measure the profitability of emotion, to determine a metric that verifies that emotion pays off for companies that invest in high-emotion strategies.

To do so, we conducted a large-scale research project that studies companies' stock performance over time. We found that emotion pays off not just in times of prosperity, but also during economic downturns!

The Index

In our study, we first surveyed the marketplace to identify firms that provide more emotion and those that provide less. We used stock market performance as our basis for comparison. Stock performance is the ultimate measure of performance for a publicly owned firm, scrutinized by those inside and outside the firm.

After collecting stock returns, we analyzed returns of the group of high-emotion firms relative to major market indices, namely the Dow, NASDAQ, and the S&P 500. In what follows, we describe the detailed results. The bottom line is that the results corroborate our theory—emotion pays off handsomely!

To compose the index we analyzed a promising set of firms. We first identified companies that, ahead of time, seemed to be likely providers of emotion. These firms were either found to have the strongest global brands (on the list of the 100 "Top Brands" as reported by *BusinessWeek* and Interbrand) or were among the most innovative (on the list of the 50 "World's Most Innovative Companies," a ranking compiled by *BusinessWeek* and Boston Consulting). Together, these lists yielded 121 unique companies. Of these, we retained consumer brands that are part of the S&P 500. For this study, only consumer product companies were considered so that we could be confident that study participants would know the companies. The result was 40 innovative companies considered strong global brands, with products and services readily recognized by U.S. consumers.

To identify which companies engender higher levels of valued emotions to their customers, we surveyed consumers to find out which of those 40 firms they believe are the ones that provide emotion. In the study, 109 respondents were asked to rate their emotional response to each firm relative to its competition. Firms were rated on a 13-point scale from weak (0) to strong (13) engendered emotion. Although all of the firms have been found either to have strong brands or to be among the most innovative (or both), the firms vary with the level of *emotion* that they engender in the respondents. The average emotion score was 8.2/13. The high-emotion firms were those for which the scores on the emotion scale were statistically greater than average, meaning that these firms delivered greater emotional benefits than the average firm that we tested. Similarly, low-emotion firms' scores were statistically lower than average, those that delivered less emotional benefit than the average firm. Both the top set and the bottom set contain firms across a range of industries: retail, software, high-technology products, fashion, and consumer packaged goods, among others.

In the analysis of stock performance, we compare the performance of higher-emotion companies to lower-emotion companies that are *within the same set of* outstanding companies (S&P 500 companies that are most innovative and/ or top brands). All of these firms are high performers, so we expect them to do quite well relative to market averages. If the higher-emotion companies outperform the others (and we find that they do), they are outperforming some of the best companies in the marketplace. Thus, we have an extremely high standard of comparison for our analysis.

This study was conducted in July 2007, so the ending point of the historical data is the end of June 2007. (For those wondering what happened during the troubled economic times that came later, we present a follow-up study later in this chapter.) The first striking aspect of the graph of three-year returns ending

FIGURE 3.1 ■ Three-year comparison of high-emotion index to others.

June 2007 (shown in Figure 3.1) is that we are remiss that we did not invest in our high-emotion index a few years before!

Of course, investing is always successful in hindsight, because it is so very easy to concoct sets of firms that performed well in the past. What we've done is different. We did not work to find a set of firms that performed well in the past. We did not use past analysis to predict future success. We developed a theory, and we are using past data to see if our theory is consistent with the stock market data. If our theory is right, higher-emotion stocks will outperform lower-emotion stocks. And that is exactly what the data shows. The high-emotion stock index exceedingly outperforms the other indices for this three-year period, by a wide margin. While the market indices (Dow Jones, S&P 500, NASDAQ) returned less than 40 percent over the three years, the high-emotion index returned greater than 100 percent.

FIGURE 3.2 ■ Ten-year comparison of high-emotion index to others.

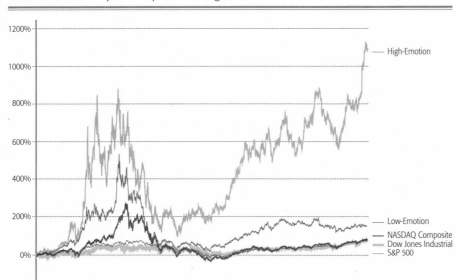

Another interesting and related result is that the low-emotion stock index underperformed the others in this three-year period, returning less than 20 percent. As with the high-emotion index, the low-emotion index is comprised of S&P 500 firms that are among the top 50 innovative companies and/or among the top 100 brands. Put differently, these are widely recognized to be outstanding companies that many people would expect to outperform market averages. In looking over a period of 10 years rather than three (see Figure 3.2), the low-emotion index did perform very well, outperforming market averages. While the low-emotion index outperformed the market averages, returning 152 percent over 10 years, the high-emotion index had exceedingly high returns of greater than 1000 percent over the same 10-year period!

These results, outstanding as they are, are worrisomely strong in their support of the value of emotion. Even though the results are consistent with what one would expect after thinking carefully about the human appreciation for emotion, are they too good to be true? Certain companies in our high-emotion index are

FIGURE 3.3 ■ Ten-year comparison of high-emotion index to others, without its highest performers.

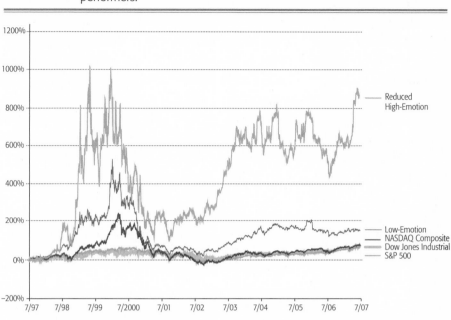

superstar stocks, in particular Apple and Google. To see if these results are due to those key firms, we also looked at the performance of the high-emotion index after omitting the superstar stocks. We found the results are not driven by a few firms, because the next 10-year performance graph (see Figure 3.3) omits the firms which appear to be in a class of their own with respect to stock performance. In Figure 3.3, the reduced high-emotion index again considerably outperformed market averages, returning around 800 percent in 10 years relative to the returns of around 70 percent from the major indices.

Even after omitting the high-flying stocks of Apple and Google, the performance of the high-emotion index remains astoundingly ahead of standard indices. No index can be such a sure bet, right? Maybe it was the timing of our study that led to such outstanding performance? The graphs in Figures 3.1–3.3 end mid-summer 2007, at that time a stock market peak. What if we did not just change the starting point (one year prior, two years prior, and so on) but also varied the ending point for the holding periods?

To change starting points and ending points, we looked at returns calculated for random buy-and-sell dates. Random buy-and-sell dates mimic what investors do in reality, because investors buy and sell on different days after holding for different amounts of time. From this viewpoint, randomizing a thousand buy-and-sell dates is the same as evaluating returns for a thousand individual investors who put their money in the market, where each investor buys and sells at random times over a 15-year period of time.

To fairly compare the performance of the high-emotion index and other standard indices, we acted as if each investor put ¼ of their money into each of the indexes: ¼ in the high-emotion index fund, ¼ in a Dow index fund, ¼ in a NASDAQ index fund, and ¼ in an S&P 500 index fund. Each individual chose his or her own buy date (a random buy date) and then bought all four funds the same day. Each individual likewise chose his or her own sell date, and sold everything at the same time. Looking at all one thousand investors with random buy-and-sell dates, we could see what percentage of investors made more money in the high-emotion index than in the standard indices.

The percentages of investors who "won" with the high-emotion index are shown in Table 3.1. It turns out that 84 percent of investors beat the Dow, 85 percent beat the NASDAQ, and 86 percent beat the S&P 500. Most investors won by investing in the high-emotion index instead of the standard indices. At the same time, these numbers are reasonable in that they show that investment in high-emotion companies is not a sure bet; for example, 16 percent of these individuals made more by investing in an index that tracks the Dow than by investing in the high-emotion companies. As must be the case, the emotion index isn't impossibly good; it does not offer guaranteed riches. Instead, we found that the high-emotion index performs very well for its investors most of the time.

Future Performance through an Economic Downturn

All the above analysis is retrospective, performed at the time we conducted our consumer survey to identify companies that engender high-value emotions, the summer of 2007. Up to that point, those companies were considered to be high-emotion companies by consumers. Would these high-emotion companies have enough staying power for the index to be predictive of future high-performing stocks?

In 2008, things changed. The world entered a deep recession and the worst economy in nearly a century. Emotion of companies is dynamic. The emotions

TABLE 3.1 ■ The percentages of investors that "win" with the high-emotion index.

Relative Performance over Random Intervals	Wins (% of investors for whom the high-emotion index yielded greater returns)
High-emotion Index vs. Dow	84%
High-emotion Index vs. NASDAQ	85%
High-emotion Index vs. S&P 500	86%

that are most highly valued in one period may be less valuable in another. In light of the dramatic economic downturn that began the following year, the natural question became how well the high-emotion index would perform through the down economy. A traditional viewpoint might have been that the high-emotion firms would underperform as the economy began to focus on the basics, eschewing unnecessary or "frivolous" emotions.

Figure 3.4 shows the performance of the stock indices for the two years subsequent to our original study. Because our original study concluded at the end of June 2007, the subsequent two years began on Monday, July 2, 2007, and ended on Tuesday, June 30, 2009. When considering the performance of the indices

FIGURE 3.4 ■ Two-year comparison of indices through the down economy.

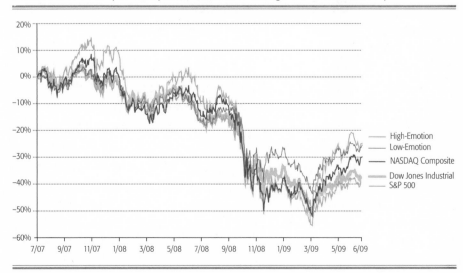

over time, there is a brief time period when the traditional viewpoint wins out. Starting in October 2008, just after the Lehmann and Goldman bankruptcy filings, the high-emotion index fell more sharply than the standard indices.

Looking at March 2009, when the market began heading upward again, the high-emotion stocks far outpaced the standard indices. Overall, looking at the two-year period in Figure 3.4, the S&P 500 lost 39.5 percent, the Dow Jones lost 37.6 percent, the NASDAQ lost 30.3 percent, but the high-emotion index lost only 25.5 percent. Through the worst U.S. economic downturn since the Great Depression, the high-emotion index fared better than the standard indices.

Also of interest in Figure 3.4 is the performance of the low-emotion index, which did very well through the worst part of the downturn. It turns out that the index did quite well because of one company that performed exceptionally well during the downturn: Wal-Mart. Clearly, there are many drivers of stock performance, including sales volume, so it comes as no surprise that Wal-Mart's stock outperformed market averages during the downturn. Yet, even with Wal-Mart, with its focus on cost and efficiency, emotions are not absent. In the economic downturn, Wal-Mart became the source of salvation for many people, where less money allowed them to still buy needs and some wants. Wal-Mart was the trusted retailer, and consumers flocked to Wal-Mart with the confidence that they were doing the best with their budgets and that they were being looked out for in the financial crunch.

What is quite clear is that Wal-Mart's stock performed quite well in relative terms, yielding a slightly positive return (0.2 percent) while stock averages lost roughly a third of their value. To assess performance of the typical low-emotion company, Figure 3.5 shows a reduced low-emotion index that omits Wal-Mart, similar to what we did earlier where we omitted Apple and Google to see the effect of these outliers on the high-emotion index.

The reduced low-emotion index still performs decently, no worse than the standard indices, but no better either. Most importantly, the high-emotion index performed quite well through the downturn, better than the full (or reduced) low-emotion index, better then the Dow, better than NASDAQ, and better than the S&P 500. Even in a down economy, emotion pays off for companies and their shareholders.

Although our stock index showed stellar past returns most of the time, the goal of our analysis was not to find a high-performing stock index. Rather,

FIGURE 3.5 ■ Two-year comparison of reduced low-emotion index to other indices through down economy.

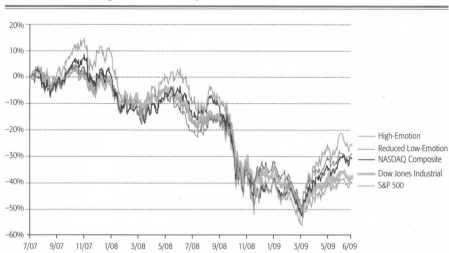

we started with a theory, and we subsequently analyzed stock performance to confirm that our theory played out in reality. Our goal was to use this study to verify in practice that it is truly profitable for companies to create products that engender positive emotional responses. We believed that if consumers value emotion, we could expect companies that provide exceptional levels of emotion to outperform those that do not. Using stock market returns, we found exactly the result that the theory would lead one to expect: high-emotion firms outperformed quality firms that deliver lower levels of emotion and the standard indices. For firms that deliver valued emotions, practice matches the theory.

The Bottom Line

Many companies make business decisions on a cost-benefit analysis. Costs should be reduced and benefits should be clearly delivered. Because emotion is intangible and difficult to convert into a dollar metric of value to the customer, it is hard to justify in the budget. It can be hard to argue the added cost on the bottom-line impact, so often that expense is removed from next year's budget. In lean times, the pressure to reduce costs is even more critical.

In our Introduction, we asked why more companies are not like Apple, why more companies don't engage customers in the experience of their product offerings, why they don't build products to be loved by their customers. The answer lies here: Most companies are paralyzed when they don't see the direct relationship between the costs and the benefits of product emotions. Apple is not. Apple drives their product development by the emotional benefits their customers receive. The result is that Apple is the most highly ranked emotion company in our index and, accordingly, has shown outstanding stock performance over an extended period of time.

This and the previous chapter have presented strong evidence that emotion pays off, that putting resources into emotion-based design is a wise decision even for those companies that count their beans. Emotion-based product development is a strategy, a long-term investment for growth. The financial benefits of emotion outweigh most costs. With this evidence in hand, management can now lead the charge to develop highly emotional, highly profitable products.

We have thus far looked at the impact of emotions at a macro level, at 30,000 feet. Now that we have demonstrated the power of emotion, we ask how your company can deliver those emotions to customers through your products. The next two chapters find that the answer lies at the micro level, the one-foot level of product features that deliver high-emotion experiences: hamburger wrappers, bright-colored power drills, tasty ice cream, and attractive gift cards. Although seemingly trivial, when carefully executed these are just some of the features that deliver high-emotion experiences that lead to profit and growth.

CHAPTER 4

The Paths to Emotion

The fundamental goal of all companies is (or should be) to provide greater value to customers. If companies successfully provide value to customers, they will also achieve all the typical business objectives, such as profitability, customer satisfaction, customer loyalty, and corporate growth.

The previous chapters described how much emotions are valued in terms of stock market performance, therefore it should be highly important to firms to provide customers with valued emotions. Yet because emotions are intangible, it may not be obvious how to build valued emotions into the product. In this and the next chapter we give company leadership two general pathways to provide emotions.

One pathway is better known, but oddly enough it's expensive and less effective. That pathway attempts to associate the product with emotions, not within the product itself but by other means, such as advertising.

The other pathway, less well-known, focuses on emotions supported and engendered by the product itself, a cost-effective strategy with long-term profit and brand benefits.

The Well-Traveled and Less-Traveled Paths

We begin with the well-traveled path, one that is closely aligned with advertising. One primary objective for advertisements is to convey information. Some ads describe a product feature ("outstanding fuel efficiency"). Some show how the focal product bests its competitors ("cleans better than the name brand"). Some highlight a current price promotion ("Labor Day weekend sale"). And some are designed simply to remind or make the viewer aware of the product ("remember our name"). Each of these kinds of advertisements conveys information, whether about product features, prices, or availability. However, not every advertisement is about information.

In the 60-second "It's Mine" Coca-Cola ad run during the 2008 Superbowl, the opening scene is an aerial view of Central Park in Manhattan, with the surrounding skyscrapers aglow in the majesty of the early morning light. The Macy's Thanksgiving Day Parade is underway along the park perimeter, and soon the ad focuses on three giant parade balloons. The center balloon is a Coca-Cola bottle, flanked by Stewie on one side and Underdog on the other, both with scowling faces.

The action of the ad is a fight between Stewie and Underdog, where they head-butt and push each other in a battle to grab the balloon bottle of Coke. Stewie, Underdog, and the Coke balloons break free from their tethering lines and begin to rise along the skyscrapers. Occasional shots show individuals from the crowd below—a flower vendor, a taxi driver, a girl reminiscent of Lucy holding a football—pausing from their work, gazing upward to see the outcome of the continuing balloon struggle. Stewie and Underdog are slowed down because they are fighting, and the bottle leaves both behind, rising above the highest buildings up into the full light of the new day. Unexpectedly, a smiling Charlie Brown balloon rises above the buildings ahead of Stewie and Underdog. Although perennial loser Charlie Brown never seems to win anything, this time he gets the prized Coke, and the ad closes with the promise of "The Coke Side of Life."

Like so many of today's advertisements, the message was not about the product features or quality. The ad did not tout the superior taste of Coke; it did not discuss its low price or its easy accessibility at the corner store. It was not compared to Pepsi, or portrayed as more refreshing. As for any information about the cola product, the advertisement was simple: There was no information at all! And yet the ad cost millions.

What the ad communicated was not information but emotion. Like many of Coke's advertisements, this one evoked satisfaction, winning, beating the norm, coming to life, freedom, and happiness. People like these feelings. Who doesn't want to feel satisfied, free, and happy? Coca-Cola provides the marketplace with a desirable cola beverage and warm emotions, and both are valued. Once the advertising has created a strong enough association of those emotions with the product, even if superficial, consumers begin to feel the emotions when they use the product.

Yet there is an even more powerful means of evoking emotions than external communications like advertising: the less-traveled path. This path does not even require a large budget, important because not all firms have a marketing budget that is anywhere near the size of Coke's! Typically overlooked, this direct and efficient path is to use the products themselves to deliver emotions.

All around us, all types of products directly deliver emotions to the marketplace, whether they are physical or software products, services, or systems. Satellite radio provides not just music and entertainment but also excitement, exploration, and, when first introduced, exclusivity. Facebook elicits a feeling of connectedness, exploration, and surprise. A BMW not only meets transportation needs, but also engenders feelings of status, success, and a daily dose of excitement; to many, it truly is the ultimate driving machine. Unlike emotions from external communications, these emotions are a part of the physical, software, or service product itself, a natural and authentic outcome of each use of the product.

A Model of the Paths to Emotion

In the Introduction to *Built to Love*, we presented a Model of the Paths to Emotion, which highlights the differences between supported and associated emotions (shown again in Figure 4.1 for reference). As briefly described earlier, there are two primary ways to deliver emotion to the marketplace: The product itself can engender emotion, or emotion can be a response to external communications such as an advertisement that describes an emotion not fully found in the product.

Emotions delivered directly by the product features are *supported emotions*. These are what we generally call "product emotions," for it is the product that delivers the emotions. Emotions created autonomously of the features of the

FIGURE 4.1 ■ A model of the Paths to Emotion: Supported emotions form products that are built to love. Associated emotions are superficial, removed from the product; some are manipulative.

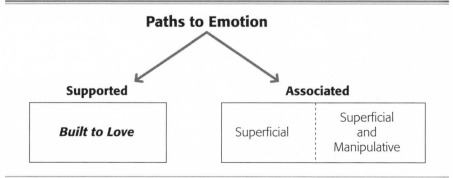

product are *associated emotions*. Because they are separate from the product, they are superficial rather than authentic to the product. Emotions created by television advertising independent of the product itself are autonomous but become linked to the product through repeated association with it. For example, Coke's "It's Mine" commercial conveys emotion and associates those emotions with the Coca-Cola product, differentiating Coke from its competitors.

In considering the difference between the two types, if there were no advertisement or other external communication for a product, what emotions would people feel? Those that they feel from the product are supported; the others are associated.

As it turns out, associated emotions have historically been the primary focus of generating emotions in customers. Because of their prominence, we consider them the well-traveled path.

Though superficial, associated emotions are not necessarily bad. However, there may be situations when associated emotions are detrimental, for example, when the company is manipulative in their presentation and use. To be manipulative is to exercise "unscrupulous control or influence over a person or situation."[8] To project fantasies is fine if they are for the good of the customer and the customer understands them to be so. Manipulative emotions are unscrupulous when they work for the welfare of the firm to the detriment of the customer.

Diet pill ads often show abnormally thin women with the claim that the pill will miraculously make you lose weight and transform you into someone else. Such advertisements are clearly manipulative because many will put their hope in the ads' claims, and typical diet pills will fail to fulfill that dream, instead contributing to a sense of failure.

Although prevalent, associated emotions typically require significant expense on the part of the firm, in that resources beyond product development must be committed to create and communicate the emotions. Because the customer does not experience these emotions when using the product until mental associations are strong, the ads or other communication means must be repeatedly shown to the potential consumer, committing the firm to ongoing expenses.

In contrast to associated emotions, supported emotions are built into the product. In this case, the power of direct interaction with the customer also avoids the high costs of associated emotions. Because people don't usually think of the product as the source of emotions, companies generally have not focused on how to design supported emotions into the product itself. Though powerful

FIGURE 4.2 ■ The Nissan Leaf.

Photos courtesy
of Nissan

and effective, this less-traveled path is under-explored and under-used, and so we have made it the focus of this book.

As an example of supported emotions, let's think about an emerging product: the electric vehicle (EV). Due to rising fuel costs and the growing impact of environmental problems with fossil fuels, more and more consumers have concerns about internal combustion engines. That, coupled with improving battery technology, is enabling EVs to become an attractive business proposition.

EVs deliver the emotional sense of independence, where the consumer is free from the constraints of fossil fuels. EVs fuel consumers' passion for improving the environment, heightening optimism that the world will become a better place. These vehicles provide drivers with joy and pride in making a difference. As long as few people have them, it also gives EV drivers the feeling of being distinct, the adventure of using something that no one else has.

Both traditional and nontraditional companies are exploring ways to introduce electric vehicles to today's marketplace. One such example is Nissan. About the time that this book is published, Nissan will be releasing their first mass-market electric vehicle in the U.S., the Leaf (see Figure 4.2). Nissan in particular has worked to advance battery technology at a cost in line with a high-volume vehicle, extending the mileage between charges. Adequate battery life is critical for giving people the confidence that they can drive throughout their normal daily activities without running out of power. The Leaf, like other EVs, is quiet, improving the environment through reduced noise pollution and fostering a feeling of serenity. The Leaf is also 99 percent recyclable, further supporting emotions about improving our world. The product itself engenders all these emotions; the emotions are supported by the product.

Additionally, there are other opportunities to build additional unique supported emotions into future electric vehicle designs. EVs don't have an engine; instead they have a big battery, so there is more space in new locations in the vehicle, providing the opportunity to reconfigure the interior space to offer drivers and passengers experiences not available in internal combustion engine vehicles today.

The marketplace has little-to-no preconceived notion of how EVs work or perform. Nissan has the opportunity in the Leaf's introduction to leverage supported emotions in its marketing, building a foundational image for the EV by engendering valued emotions that the car authentically provides. The supported emotions do not need to be used alone; supported and associated emotions can be coordinated to be used in concert, not simply as individual strategies. Associated emotions that echo the supported ones, such as projecting a clean and quiet world for and from the EV vehicle, will amplify reality, helping users feel more proud, passionate, optimistic, and independent.

There is enormous potential in supported emotions. Ads will still be valuable in that they create awareness of a product and its benefits, both functional and emotional. Not all ads are based strictly on associated emotions (though many are). An ad may also communicate the supported emotions. Either way, it is the supported emotions that feed long-term customer satisfaction, especially in our current marketplace where many consumers pay more attention to raw online user reviews than to carefully crafted, on-screen messaging. Supported emotions are authentic, delivering to customers what the product truly provides. A smart business choice, they are cost effective to manage and produce.

This book is primarily about supported emotions because for many markets and products supported emotions remain an untapped opportunity for profits and customer satisfaction. The remaining focus of this chapter, however, is on associated emotions. We will look at their power, and the danger of their use when independent of supported emotions. The following chapters will focus on the use of supported emotions.

The Well-Traveled Path: Associated Emotions

Of the two types of emotions, supported and associated, it is the associated emotions that are most familiar to companies and the general public, possibly due to the prevalence of advertising. If designed well, they supplement and augment the fundamental value of the product. The happiness of Charlie Brown's smile augments the

Coke product, associating Coke and happiness. Over time, with enough investment in creating such associations through advertising, associated emotions can be powerful, as evidenced by the success of Coca-Cola. Associated emotions are commonly used for purchase motivation, to help create awareness of those products that are newer or lesser-known, to move the potential customer from awareness to interest, from interest to desire, then from desire to the action of buying.

Associated emotions can be seemingly unrelated to the product. Think about a Coke's emotion, such as the feeling of American-style freedom. That feeling of freedom doesn't come from the water, the primary ingredient of Coke. Water is real, but it's not the "real thing." Nor does the feeling of freedom come from the carbonation, the flavoring, or even from the caffeine. The feeling of freedom is a completely new creation of the advertising. Advertising associates emotions with products, connecting to emotional longings such as the desires to be accepted, to escape the mundane tedium of everyday life, or to experience the "Coke side of life."

Frequently the emotions in advertisements have a connection to at least some product attributes. Some emotions established early on for Coke did relate to product attributes. When Coke was introduced, it had cocaine as one of its ingredients, providing supported emotions of satisfaction and happiness (and wanting more). When Coca-Cola removed cocaine early in the twentieth century, they leveraged the remaining caffeine to promote satisfaction and happiness.

If introduced today, it is unclear whether Coke could build up such a strong brand purely with advertising because of the expense as well as the desire of customers for authenticity in advertising. Coke has been advertising for decades, and consumers do feel a sense of satisfaction and happiness when drinking a Coke, not just when viewing an advertisement for Coke. As we will demonstrate soon, Coke and other colas actually elicit emotion even in blind taste tests. But the emotional difference among various colas is slight when consumers are not told what brand they are drinking, leaving Coke's success to a loyal customer base and a highly successful but quite costly ad campaign.

Many advertised emotions connect to product attributes for other products as well. Advertisements for International Coffee promise a break from the mundane, the essence of a European café. Although functionally it is a flavored instant coffee that takes you no closer to Europe than wherever you are drinking it, its non-standard and rich flavors are a break from the ordinary, giving some credence to the promise of an emotional escape. Or consider IBM's promise of connectivity for your business to anywhere and everywhere in the world. Although no company needs to be connected literally everywhere, the promise has value.

Similarly, SUVs often suggest the freedom of navigating the great outdoors. Even if used only on suburban roads, the capabilities and features of off-road SUVs allow the driver to navigate roads that are inaccessible with cars, supporting emotions of power over the surroundings, freedom from the constraints of pavement, and adventure of exploration of new terrain. Although some SUVs are clearly designed for suburban families to shuttle between soccer matches and supermarkets with somewhat limited clearance and limited off-pavement capabilities, the citified SUV is part of an SUV family and visually looks akin to its off-road cousins. The emotion of freedom is enabled in part by its visual appearance as an SUV.

In light of the nature of SUVs, advertisements for SUVs often show vehicles in extreme conditions, sometimes to show their capabilities (for example, the ability to climb steep hills); at other times they convey emotions of adventure and power (the SUV pictured atop a mesa). Such advertisements are natural ones to show because the emotions in them build off of those that are supported by the product itself. Although it is possible to create associated emotions that have no connection to or resonance from product attributes, often the emotions created by advertising and other communications have some link to those attributes, blurring the line between associated and supported emotions.

In the case of SUVs, the extreme situations shown in the advertisements may be misleading if exaggerated beyond what the product supports. SUVs cannot actually climb mesas and many have such low clearance that they could not go far off-road. Safety may be the largest reason that people buy SUVs, but extreme ads make for more exciting viewing. As ads begin to deviate from the reality of functional (and emotional) capabilities, the ads become misleading. Associated emotions are most useful, with long-term benefits, when they truly echo the emotions delivered by the product or build up fantasies in a straightforward and open way.

One can think of advertising as asking questions that will be answered by the product. A makeup commercial that portrays the emotion of self-confidence asks, "Don't you want to be beautiful? To be confident in your appearance?" The make-up product itself delivers the beauty, answering the hope from the commercial, offering the wearer the ability to say, "I am now beautiful." The associated emotion of the advertisement anticipates emotions of the product, asking the questions to be answered by the product, clearly implying if not directly stating that the product will fulfill the desires evoked by the advertisement.

A problem is that many products do not fulfill all that has been claimed about them. Similar to those diet pills that promise more than delivered, an advertisement for makeup can exaggerate its ability to transform a person. The power of advertising has, at times, led to misuse of associated emotions, where they were employed to manipulate and persuade customers rather than to inform and to benefit them. When advertisements claim more than what the product actually delivers, the product ends up being hollow, without appropriate substance behind it. Chrysler's claim to high-quality manufacture in the 1990s, in contrast to the realities of the finished product, disappointed some customers, hurting Chrysler's brand and contributing to a poor emotional experience for those customers.

Of course, if the product supports the advertised emotions, the claims ring true because they are borne out. The claims are authentic. How might a weight-loss product, for example, authentically support the consumer, using the product to create emotions that can be truly delivered? As an answer, consider a different diet "pill" introduced in 2007 in the U.S. by GlaxoSmithKline. Currently the only over-the-counter weight loss product that has FDA approval, Alli is working for the good of its customers instead of manipulating them. Alli delivers no fantasy. Instead, Alli provides weight loss guidance by teaching users how to moderate their diet, while at the same time it reduces their fat intake. Alli prevents about 25 percent of the fat that users eat from being absorbed by their bodies. They can eat whatever they want, but there is a limit. If they exceed a certain amount of fat intake at any meal, typically 15 grams, the user may spend extra time in the bathroom. The user quickly understands their limit and they change their eating habits. To help users change their habits to adopt a healthy lifestyle, GlaxoSmithKline's "product" is more than the pill. The product also includes an education guide, access to a website, and the possibility of buying a magazine for the healthy-weight person. Alli's ads are factual yet optimistic, engendering only emotions supported by the pill and its related products and services. For example, the ads show elation, where the elation is the joy that the user experiences after diligently working to lose weight. Fulfillment, confidence, pride, and optimism are other emotions felt by the successful Alli user.

Supported emotions are by definition authentic, because they are not empty claims but are actually fulfilled by the product. A safe route for advertising is to evoke those emotions that are legitimately supported, in which case customers will experience the promise fulfilled.

The Value of Associated Emotions

Although this book emphasizes the powerful role of supported emotions, it is important to understand associated emotions, to recognize how they work, and to assess their influence on product value. In the case of associated emotions, their influence comes through word and image. Can emotion-laden words by themselves add value to a product?

To answer this question, we ran a study that investigates the impact of just a single superficial word on the value of a product, where 75 people were given a description about goose-down fill, the insulating material in winter coats. Two different down fills were described in two different coats. One was "regular" down fill and the other was "Alpine" down fill. Study participants were told that the down fill in both coats offered the exact same performance and quality. An earlier survey showed that the word "Alpine" would connote the thrill of adventure and other similar emotions, while the term "regular" is generic.[9] In our study, subjects were asked to evaluate their emotion in response to these different down-filled coats, where the coats were identical except for the two descriptor terms for the down fill (Alpine and regular). Before we get to the results, let's ask what kinds of emotions down-filled coats might evoke. For outdoor coats for extremely cold weather, coats may evoke feelings of independence because customers may feel the freedom to venture outdoors, or coats may evoke feelings of adventure in the context of outdoor sports, or coats may evoke feelings of power because the wearer is able to be reasonably comfortable despite the weather. Additionally, coats are clothing, and all clothing contributes to image, evoking the possibility of many more emotions (for example, feelings of distinctiveness or luxuriousness).

The study results were striking. Relative to the label "regular" for the down fill, the simple use of the label "Alpine" led respondents to feel more distinctive, adventurous, independent, sensuous, proud, passionate, and powerful than regular down fill. All of that emotion was created by just a single word!

Labels matter not just for relatively expensive items like coats but also for very inexpensive items, like pasta. We ran a similar study[10] with describing words on pasta, using the labels "regular pasta" and "Authentic Milanese pasta." Again, the 80 subjects were told that this was the same quality pasta, and the only difference communicated was the descriptor terms. The results were just like those for the down fill, where simple verbal descriptions yielded different emotional responses. Like "Alpine" for down fill, "Authentic Milanese" for pasta yielded greater emotional value relative to "regular" pasta.

Associated emotions can thus be evoked even by well-chosen words.

Neuroscience and Associated Emotions

Recent research has investigated the extent to which associated emotions are truly felt by consumers. One study, published in the *Proceedings of the National*

FIGURE 4.3 ■ Wine is a highly emotional product.

Photo by Melissa Cagan

Academy of Sciences,[11] measured the study participants' emotional reactions to prices of wines that they tasted as part of the study. The participants were instructed that they were sampling five different Cabernet Sauvignons. While tasting the wines, participants were shown retail prices of the wines, which ranged from $5 to $90 per bottle. Participants were asked to rate each wine on "taste pleasantness."

In truth, there were not five wines but three. Each participant tasted two of the wines twice, but at different prices, and in random orders. One of the wines was presented as both the $5 wine and the $45 wine. Another was presented as both the $10 and the $90 wine. A third wine was tasted at a price of $35.

The results of this part of the study were in line with findings of previous experiments, where participants claimed to enjoy the higher-priced wines more than the lower-priced wines. There have been various explanations for this kind of outcome, which is that higher-priced items tend to be judged as higher quality. The most pervasive explanation is simply that people believe higher-priced items should be higher quality. For this study, that explanation would imply that participants who are not wine experts believe the higher-priced wine should taste better, and they then report what they believe the answers should be rather than their true assessment of what they tasted. One implication of this result is that participants' self-reported taste ratings should not be viewed as reliable, because their ratings appear to be influenced by price and not solely by taste.

With today's technology, respondents' brains can be scanned and analyzed with functional magnetic resonance imaging (fMRI). The fMRI allows researchers to measure activity in different portions of the brain. For example, wine tastes would be expected to lead to higher brain activity in the medial orbitofrontal cortex (mOFC), an area of the brain that is widely thought to encode for actual experienced pleasantness. In brief, the fMRI allows the researchers to look beyond the self-reported scores of the wine study participants and assess what they really felt about the wine, not what they reported themselves to feel.

For anyone who does not recognize the value of associated emotions, the results were shocking. Brain activity was compared for the two pairs of identical wines, comparing the $5 brain scans to those of the $45 wine, and comparing the $10 brain scans with those of the $90 wine. Both comparisons yielded the same results: Brain scans of the mOFC showed that respondents actually enjoyed the wine more at the higher price.

Importantly, scans of the primary taste regions of the brain, such as the insula cortex and the ventroposterior medial nucleus of the thalamus, were unaffected by the price variation. Put differently, respondents' brains were accurate on the actual taste, not detecting any difference in flavor of identical wines.

The fMRI technology validated what the respondents had been saying all along with simple paper-and-pencil quality ratings: They truly did enjoy higher-priced wines more. Putting together the various scans of the brain in this study, the results showed that participants were reasonably accurate in assessing the taste of wines. At the same time, there was an emotional component based on associated emotions that added value above and beyond the taste because the higher prices on wines led participants to derive more pleasure from the wine tastes.

It is important to note that the participants did not pay for the wine, nor were they asked what they would pay for it. The price on the bottle did not necessarily reflect the amount they would be willing to pay for the additional emotion. The message of the study is not that increasing the price of a product will lead to increased profits or increased value. What the study does tell us is that associated emotions are real and, in the right context, can increase the emotional value of a product.

The Love of Commodities

By now you are pretty well convinced that the value of emotion is pervasive, and you may be hoping to find ways to build emotion into your company's products. You've seen that emotion is valued by people regardless of whether they are buying consumer products for themselves or seemingly purely functional products for their companies. Then, just as you are thinking of ways to add emotion, you remember that your industry is cutthroat competitive, that your company and your competitors have very similar products, and that your customers seem to be focused on price alone. Is there room to add emotion into highly price-oriented markets?

We looked at products that have found differentiation in the market, products that if separated from their brand names would be commodities. These products are so common and cost-driven that emotion would seem to be irrelevant. We conducted a set of studies to look at both supported and associated emotion in a few common food items, considering whether salsas, colas, and vanilla ice creams elicited any emotions, and which emotions. Although brands can be strongly emotional, do the products evoke emotions by themselves when brand names are removed? We wondered whether salsas might elicit some emotion due to their spiciness, and whether colas might have some effect due to the caffeine. Vanilla ice cream is just that (vanilla), but maybe the decadence of ice cream creates emotion even for plain vanilla. These foods were chosen because supported and associated emotions could be isolated and compared to one another.

For these product categories, supported emotions are those that the product (for example, cola) evokes, while associated emotions are those evoked by individual brands (like Pepsi). In the part of the study focused on supported emotions, participants sampled foods without being shown the brands. First, 21 participants were asked to rate three unbranded salsas, three unbranded colas, and three unbranded ice creams. The brands were hidden and even the shape of the containers was not shown. In each food category, a local supermarket product (generic private label) was used along with two national brands. Prior to evaluating how each of these products made the subjects feel, and between each sample of food or drink, the participants ate a table water cracker and drank water to cleanse the palate. We used a variation of a tool called the eMap, discussed in Chapter 6, to analyze specific emotions stimulated by the foods. Results are seen in the charts of Figure 4.4.

It was striking that participants responded emotionally even to the unbranded foods. As for emotions that were statistically significant in the study,

FIGURE 4.4 ■ Emotion Maps (eMaps) of emotions of unbranded foods. Note that when no brand is shown these products become commodities with little differentiation. Yet even the unbranded products still demonstrate emotions to those who consume them.

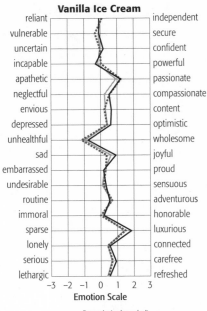

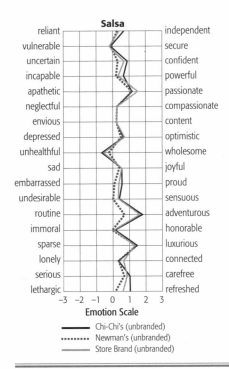

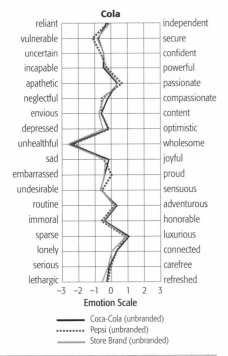

FIGURE 4.5 ■ Three ice creams, salsas, and colas used in the study.

Photos by Ying Lee

all three of the food categories elicited a feeling of luxuriousness. In addition, salsa made people feel passionate. The emotions evoked by the foods were not just desirable emotions. All three foods gave people the feeling of unhealthiness, although colas were particularly negative on feelings of health. Given cola's popularity, it was interesting to see that many emotions scored in the negative range for colas. Of particular note, some of the negative scores indicated that people felt unhealthful, insecure, and undesirable. With the exception of giving people the feeling of unhealthiness, salsas and ice creams generally elicited positive emotions across the board.

What is so interesting is that basic commodities—basic foods—actually elicit supported emotions when eaten. These are the baseline emotions for the product categories, regardless of brand. When branding and/or advertising add in associated emotions, the overall net emotion felt by the customer shifts. If baseline emotions are negative, as is especially the case for colas, positive associated emotions from the brand need to outweigh the negative feelings from the product, so that the consumers feel great about the product.

To better understand this, 20 different participants were next given the same test, but this time the brands were revealed (see Figure 4.5). The emotions of the product categories were on average the same as in the previous test. However, here we were also able to look at emotional differences between the brands within the categories, as shown in Figure 4.6.

Chi Chi's salsa brand scored well on multiple positive emotions and was particularly strong in adventure and confidence. Newman's, which also scored well for many emotions, was especially strong for adventure and luxuriousness. Either one of these brands gives the buyer a good-tasting salsa and also imparts multiple positive feelings associated with their purchase; both outperformed the generic counterpart. Ironically, the same generic salsa had stronger supported emotions than the Newman's salsa in the unbranded study. Brands of ice cream similarly differentiated on emotion. Thus, emotion, not just product attributes such as flavors, can be used to differentiate brands.

Interestingly, the store brand evoked almost no positive emotional response at all in any of the product categories. While store brands have made huge strides in product quality in recent years, this result indicates that store brands could benefit from an investment in emotional value in order to be emotionally embraced by consumers. Especially in product categories for which the baseline is negative, such as for colas, store brands must offer positive emotions to offset and outweigh the baseline emotions. Thinking back to the "Authentic Milanese" versus regular pasta study, such branding could shift consumer emotions. Such branding exercises are being seen in chain supermarkets today.

To stand out in a commoditized category you must do something different. This is especially so in categories like colas, where players have established their brands over a long time. One that did just that is Jolt Cola. First introduced in 1985 in Rochester, New York, home of the company, Jolt claimed to have "all the sugar and twice the caffeine" as other colas, standing out as an early energy drink.

Among ice creams, Ben and Jerry's created unique-sounding flavors, full of chunks of chocolate and other goodies, to stand apart in the ice cream market. Providing further emotion to customers through activist commitments, the company established a unique path among a commoditized field.

Emotion is unavoidably present, found even in highly competitive, cost-oriented product categories where it is relatively simple to make the product itself. Here, where there is very little differentiation between the actual products, emotional value provides the opportunity for differentiation. With a convincing enough advertising campaign, emotions that are not even supported can be associated so strongly to the product as to be powerful. Coke and Pepsi together hold about 75 percent of the market share of colas, even though there are countless local brands of colas. The strength of Coke and Pepsi is heavily driven by associated

FIGURE 4.6 ■ Emotion Maps (eMaps) of emotions of branded foods. The brands cause emotion differentiation among the products, separating the branded product from a commoditized product.

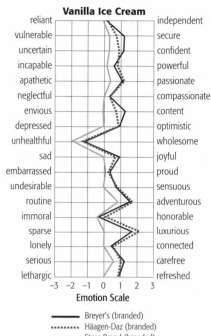

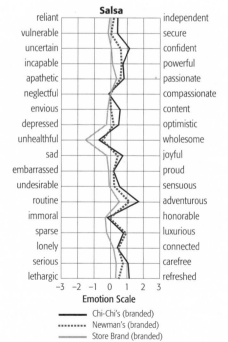

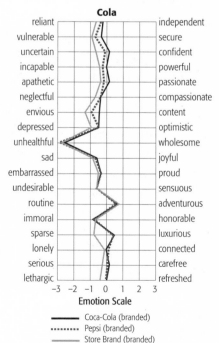

emotions, for, despite a strongly held belief among consumers that they are driven by the flavor of the products, blind taste tests with full-calorie colas typically show that only the cola aficionados care about the difference in taste between Coke (or Pepsi) and its store-brand competitors. Even considering Coke versus Pepsi, where the taste difference is more noticeable, think about your own experience. Imagine you are at a restaurant with friends, and when one of your friends orders Coke, the waitress tells him that they only have Pepsi. She asks him whether he would like Pepsi instead. What do you think your friend would do: order Pepsi or a different drink? What would you do in this situation? In a study of 130 participants where these two questions were asked, 88 percent expected their friend to order Pepsi instead, and 84 percent would also choose Pepsi themselves.[12]

Despite little difference in the actual cola products, the emotional differences are real and valued by consumers, even if superfluous. Think about what would happen if there were *no* differences in emotional value of colas: Everyone would begin buying the local store-brand cola after participating in a taste test. In fact, they may even be angry at the national brands for fooling them all these years, forcing customers to pay a higher price for a product that tastes the same as the local competitor. But that is not what happens.

We've run blind taste tests. Consumers are not angry at all when they find out that Coke tastes the same as a local store brand. They are surprised, somewhat amused, but not angry at all. At the end of one of our studies, after clearly showing a group that they could not tell the difference between Coke and the local generic store brand in terms of taste alone, participants were told that they could take the unfinished liter bottles with them if they wanted. All of the Coke was taken; all of the store-brand cola was left behind. Clearly, people celebrate Coke for more than its taste. Charlie Brown in the "It's Mine" ad, and the rest of the advertisements purchased by the hundreds of millions of dollars that Coke and Pepsi spend annually, generate emotional value to create perceived differentiation among commoditized products: value made real. But it does cost them hundreds of millions of dollars to do so.

Where to Put Your Money: Costs of Associated versus Supported Emotions

Emotion is valuable, but what does it cost to evoke emotion? Associated emotions, through traditional communication such as advertising, can be extremely expensive, prohibitively so for all but the largest firms. Because the product itself does not evoke these emotions, the expense of associated emotions is ongoing. Coke, for example, is reported to spend well over $200 million per year for media in the U.S. for Coca-Cola trademarked products alone.

Advertisements must do more than simply make claims of associated emotions: The claims must be believable. Otherwise, the intended emotion is dismissed and ignored rather than evoked. The most obvious examples of believable associated emotions are for products from those companies that have spent decades at the task. Coke, founded over 100 years ago, has had a century of investment in associated emotions. Today, Coke truly does elicit a youthful happiness. For new brands and new products, there is a risk in attempting to create associated emotions, a risk that the planned investment level in advertising or other communications will not be sufficient to create the required legitimacy and authenticity of those emotions. Worse yet, claimed but unfulfilled associated emotions may cloud or dilute the rest of the value proposition of the product.

In contrast, products that deliver supported emotions directly do the work of advertising without the cost of advertising. When a product evokes desired emotions, those emotions make a happy customer, literally. More formally, the emotions heighten customer satisfaction and create loyalty because customers feel great about the product. Customers aren't ambivalent about the product; they love it! Loyalty and emotion run together: Krispy-Kreme fanatics are both loyal and passionate about the brand, Apple fanatics are both loyal and passionate about the brand, Harley fanatics are both loyal and passionate about the brand. When the product directly delivers the emotions, the product itself leads to passion, and passion leads to loyalty. The fanaticism about Apple was not the outcome of a coordinated effort for hype, but it was the result of emotion created by its products.

It is the same story for Harley, Krispy-Kreme, and Starbucks, companies that rose to prominence with almost no national advertising. Their products delivered valued emotions, and those emotions fueled the loyalty that was the first element that propelled the rapid growth of these firms. Relying on a strategy of supported emotions rather than associated emotions, these companies' products are built to love, and customers do love their products.

Truth in Advertising

A vast industry has been built up around advertising. The industry is critical to many companies, by informing the marketplace of new products, of changes to existing products, of promotions, or of how one product compares to another. As demonstrated in this chapter, advertisements serve more than an informational role, for associated product emotions can magnify the sales potential of a product. However, the potential influence of associated emotions on product sales has a downside.

Associated emotions that echo the product's supported emotions can magnify the customer's emotional connection to the product, reinforcing the benefits that customers receive from the product. This is true for all products but especially critical for the overall brand, which influences perception of portfolios of individual products. When the associated emotions are counter to the actual supported emotions the overall effect is confusion, disappointment, and, at times, anger and potential disdain for a product.

As with other aspects of life, trust in a product (including a brand) is built over time, and one dishonest interaction can wreak tremendous damage. The misuse of associated emotions can result in a loss of the customers' trust in a product. Companies, and the people that work within, have a fundamental responsibility to treat others fairly, openly, and with compassion, and not doing so will result in an eventual loss of customer loyalty.

Associated emotions have an additional role: projecting a product as a part of people's fantasies. We are not against this purpose. We are not suggesting that those of you who watch the Superbowl only for the ads will have to start watching reruns on other channels out of boredom. Exciting, engaging, and entertaining ads bring enjoyment and satisfy a need, helping people project who they are and what they want to be. Successful fantasy-based commercials are honest because the viewer understands them to be fantasies or exaggerations. The intent should be to entertain and inform and not mislead, and the product itself should not disappoint advertising claims. The ad should not be designed to help the company at the expense of the customer; it should be designed to the benefit of both customer and company. To do so, the ad should leverage and build upon emotions that are actually engendered by the product, emotions that help people fulfill their desires and dreams.

Next, Chapter 5 digs deeper into supported emotions, looking at the emotions they engender, their impact on potential profit, and a few examples of emotions that you might not have considered.

CHAPTER **5**

Supported Emotions:
The Key to Today's Leading Products

Unlike commonly found associated emotions, the less frequently used supported emotions are delivered by the product itself, evoked by features or attributes of the physical product, software, service, or brand. Today's marketplace is looking for an authentic relationship with its products. Supported emotions are the only means to deliver that authentic relationship.

Supported emotions result in high customer engagement and they also get customers talking. Those who own the product talk to their friends or write on their blogs because customers talk about what moves them at an emotional level. The word spreads. Word-of-mouth offers the potential for exponential sales growth as each customer talks to a few friends, some of whom buy the product, get the emotional benefits and become passionate, and in turn talk to new friends. The reputation builds with experiences that get talked about.

Paraphrasing *Field of Dreams*, people will come if you successfully build it; here, the word spreads due to the passion that your product creates. It is more than a task fulfilled; rather, an emotional experience has been created. People will come back for the satisfaction of the delivered emotions, wanting more.

As an additional benefit to companies that deliver supported emotions, these firms do not need a large marketing budget. Product success from supported emotions is often achieved with relatively little expense on the part of the firm.

Each feature and detail of a product offers an opportunity to deliver emotions that resonate with customers. Consider the iconic, emotive, high-tech company Apple, and how the details of its physical and virtual products and services work together to create emotions. Apple heavily utilizes supported emotions with products that not only fulfill needs but also excite the customer. In every product that Apple produces, the interface, performance, clever software, integration, and advanced contemporary design work together to deliver valued emotions to customers.

For Apple, supported emotions have produced a fanatical following of satisfied and repeat customers. Apple's customers are fanatical because the company made them that way, repeatedly and consistently delivering desirable emotional experiences with their products. Apple is consistent in using products to deliver both function and emotion, whether the product is the iPod, iPhone, iPad, a desktop or laptop computer, the software that runs on those computers, or customer service.

It's All in the Numbers

Consider an Apple software product as an example of how it delivers both supported emotion and function. Apple's software suite called "iWork" is an alternative to Microsoft's Office suite which was designed for home use and small business customers. The newest member of the iWork suite is Numbers, the Excel of iWork. Although not as comprehensive as Excel in terms of the number of pre-programmed functions, Numbers meets the performance needs of most users with over 150 mathematical functions.

Numbers also goes beyond functional needs in the Apple way. Numbers provides a user-friendly, easy-to-use, understandable interface and foundation to make spreadsheet calculations a welcome and effective part of everyday information tasks. For small businesses this includes financial reporting, ROI calculations, and invoicing. For personal financial tasks this includes a plan for college savings, elementary school homework assignments, and even wedding planning! Numbers goes beyond the blank spreadsheet by providing templates that are aesthetically pleasing, stylistically appropriate, and preloaded with hidden formulas that address what is typically a tedious part of life. Calculation is turned into an enjoyable and intuitive experience. Numbers rethinks expectations in how to approach and use a spreadsheet. And it's easy to personalize any use by dragging in photos from iPhoto (integrating it into the Apple software system) or the Internet.

How do users react to Numbers? Reviews not only discuss the functionality of Numbers, but Numbers elicited an emotional reaction as well: "Numbers is elegant", "no-brainer," "helps you think outside the grid," "pleases the eye," "amazing," "a killer app," "unlike any other spreadsheet tool," "so cool" (followed by astonishment that the reviewer actually thought of a spreadsheet application as "cool"), "great and inspiring." One reviewer said, "If you're a Mac user, take the trial for a spin. If you're a Windows user, I'm sorry, you're just going to have to drool jealously."[13]

All of these comments are positive, but that isn't our point. We want you to notice that Numbers clearly engenders emotional reactions, fitting the consistent pattern of Apple's successful delivery of supported emotions to its user base that fulfill emotional value through their products and product features.

The Value of Supported Emotions

Chapter 3 established the value of emotions provided by a company or brand. How about the emotion of an individual product, or even the emotion delivered by an individual product feature or detail? Is there emotional resonance with the micro level of product details just like at the macro level of corporate brands?

If we break apart the gestalt of a product into individual components, we can consider each component's emotional contribution to product satisfaction and profit. Consider Apple at the detail level. Apple designs the emotional experience at a level of detail that few other companies even pay attention to. Recognizing that their showrooms make a first emotional impression on potential customers by providing an impressive and engaging experience, their stores go beyond the function of presenting wares. The stores are meticulously organized, spacious, with contemporary design, soft wood, and crisp lines. Energetic, professionally competent yet casually dressed employees greet you, assist you, teach you, and, if you need it, engage you at the "Genius Bar" for technical support.

Similarly, Apple's website features the latest innovations, supports easy-to-follow educational and demonstration videos, includes blogs to answer questions and address product issues, and provides an informative virtual store. A physical visit to the store or a virtual visit to the website empowers and excites the customer, giving both information and emotions, such as the confidence to make informed purchases in a complex and sometimes bewildering technical world.

For many companies, offering customers enticing experiences ends with the showroom, while Apple goes further, investing in seemingly mundane details beyond the showroom experience. Think about its investment in product packaging, for example. Packaging not only protects the product during shipment, but it can offer the customer an emotional experience while opening the packaging to find the gem inside: in Apple's case, the new iPhone, iMac, or iPad.

Apple has deliberately invested in the details of its product packaging. But why? Why devote so much expense to a functional, seemingly unimportant aspect of product delivery that will be immediately disposed of by most customers? Clearly, Apple believes that its investment in packaging pays off in some fashion, but does the investment in such a minor detail really translate into a noticeably improved emotional experience, or, better yet, higher profit margins?

FIGURE 5.1 ■ Apple packaging stands out. Thinkpad box (left) versus the MacBook box (right).

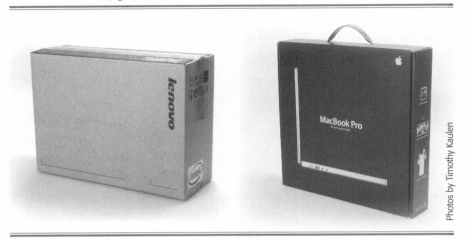

Photos by Timothy Kaulen

To see whether emotion is valued in product features, we need to separate it from other features and evaluate it independently. Otherwise, one can always argue that the product's success comes from other attributes such as stellar functionality, for instance, that the success of Apple isn't from emotion at all but rather from its logical interface and technical performance.

In the following study, we focus on packaging, an individual component that can be tested for its emotional contribution to product satisfaction and profit. We consider whether packaging influences how much a consumer values a product, and we assess whether an investment in packaging is worth the expense. The goal of showing this study is to understand how product features can make a difference in emotional satisfaction and willingness to pay for a product, even for product features such as packaging that are seemingly distant or irrelevant.

As you think about this study, recognize that this really isn't about packaging but about proving that emotion at the feature level impacts the success of the overall product. This study is about recognizing that emotion pays. In our study,[14] 123 graduate students were offered a mug with the emblem of their university (see Figure 5.2). About half the students received the mug in an ordinary brown cardboard packing box, and the rest of the students received the mug in an appealing, black gift box. After receiving the mug, the students stated how much the mug was worth to them and they had the opportunity to sell the mug back to us at or above the amount that they stated.

FIGURE 5.2 ■ The ordinary box, the mug, and the appealing box for the packaging study.

Photos by Timothy Kaulen

What was interesting was that the students who received the mug in the appealing gift box valued the mug more highly (required more money to sell back the mug) than those who received the exact same mug in the cardboard packing box. The difference was statistically significant and profitable. The more appealing black box increased the value by $0.82 above the value of the mug in the cardboard box, yet the appealing black box cost only $0.50 more than the ordinary cardboard box (a 64 percent margin).

The simple detail of an appealing box as opposed to an ordinary box made students attach greater value to the mug. Maybe this is so surprising that one might argue that something other than emotion was what was valued, for example, that the black gift box could be reused for gifts, a convenient way to package Aunt Mary's holiday present. Thus the box would be more valuable not because of emotion but because it had a second use.

To address this skeptical but reasonable rebuttal, we ran a second study, one where the packaging was a paper card and envelope that was essentially useless when opened. We attached $25 gift cards for Panera Bread on the paper cards that were placed in the envelopes, resulting in the packaging having trivial value afterwards. About half the students received a gift card in a plain envelope/paper card package, and the rest received the gift card in a more appealing matching stationary card and envelope. The more appealing, higher-quality, green envelope and paper was thicker and textured, while the plain packaging consisted of a white index card in a plain white business envelope. Clearly, the packaging had no significant further use.

Both groups of students, 132 undergraduates in all, were asked the same question: How much would you pay for the card? One might imagine that a $25 gift card is equivalent to $25 in cash. However, many issues affected how much the students were willing to pay. These included convenience (getting to Panera to use the card), desire (whether they liked Panera), and income (these were students so they might have been more careful on how much of their available cash they precommitted to spending at one retailer). Each of these issues might have been a reason why students would pay less than $25 for the card.

The results of the gift card study yielded the same story as the mug study. Students who viewed the Panera card in the more appealing packaging were on average willing to pay $21.28 for the $25 card, while the card in the plain package resulted in a willingness to pay of only $18.98. The more appealing packaging led students to be willing to pay an extra $2.30, while the more appealing packaging cost only $0.40 more (a margin now of 475 percent!). All of these results are statistically significant, meaning they are solid and may be generalized to similar situations outside of the study.

The experiments showed that an investment in packaging could increase customers' willingness to pay above and beyond the incremental cost of the packaging. In the second study, the packaging had no significant value after the product was removed, thus proving that the packaging's contribution to value was not its own potential future use. To confirm that the value from the package was driven by emotion, the students in the latter study were given a questionnaire that measured the emotions the packaging engendered in them. Positive emotions were significantly higher for the appealing packaging relative to the ordinary packaging, supporting the contention that emotion drove the value up for the card.

The point of these studies is not to argue that companies should focus on improving packaging (although that is clearly one potential implication). The broader point is that every detail of a product can be used to provide valued emotions. If a trivial feature such as packaging can have such a significant effect on the emotional response and willingness to pay for a product, it should be clear that more critical and permanent features of the product could have an equivalent or greater impact on customer experience.

The features highlighted here and elsewhere in the book are part of the fulfillment of overall emotion-based opportunities. Targeting a single feature independent of an overall product may or may not provide overall emotional benefits to the product. Simply putting a product in glitzy packaging will likely not be enough to achieve the much greater opportunity. Each feature should be designed to contribute to the emotional value of the product, in concert with its other features.

B-to-B Emotions

Since you have read this far, perhaps you now believe, or want to believe, that at least *some* people value emotions and are willing to pay for products that offer those emotions. Which people? In what contexts do people seek emotions? How about purchasers of business-to-business products who are not even going to use the products themselves? What if the product is purely functional, like a copper water pipe or a drill bit; do buyers value emotional aspects of these products or product parts?

Maybe emotion is relevant to Apple because Apple is primarily selling to consumers rather than to businesses, and maybe it is easy to find emotion with Apple because computers are no longer just back-office machines but emotion-laden entertainment centers? Does the potential for a company to provide emotion exist for the experience of using functional products in the business-to-business (B-to-B) environment?

At face value, it would seem that the B-to-B market is immune to the appeal of emotion, because businesses would only consider "real" aspects of products as opposed to fluffy, ephemeral emotions. In a business-based purchasing environment, expenses must be justified by product performance, and one might be tempted to believe that business buyers would avoid emotions due to extra costs (assuming there are extra costs). Businesses are rational and calculating, not seduced by the emotional deliverables of a product, right? Well, actually, wrong.

To assess the relevance of emotion for products in general, let's look at the extreme case: a truly functional product in a business-to-business context. Consider the potential for emotion in a flexible pipe for natural gas, a commercial product that is rarely seen after installation. Just as in a household, gas appliances in commercial kitchens must connect to the gas line on the wall. Dormont Manufacturing, a relatively small company headquartered in western Pennsylvania, is the leading provider of utility connections between commercial appliances (such as stoves and ovens) and the gas lines in restaurants. Known as the "Blue Hose" due to their blue color, and trademarked as such, Dormont's gas connectors are flexible, allowing kitchen workers to pull a gas appliance out from the wall in order to clean underneath and behind the appliance. Clearly, safety is the number one goal of such a product. There are many competitors in the market who meet safety standards, but Dormont's Blue Hose stands out against the competition.

With the myriad of decisions to be made in designing and constructing commercial kitchens, the Blue Hose provides builders and kitchen-facilities designers one part for which no decision needs to be made. For over 30 years, the Blue Hose has met or exceeded quality standards and safety regulations. Rather than investigate regulations and evaluate which products are appropriate, designers and builders rely on Dormont to meet regulations regardless of whether the directive is generated by a local municipality, a fire marshal, or by the federal government.

In a product area where safety standards are highly important, and where there are myriad regulations that vary not just by country or state but by local municipalities, Dormont offers peace of mind to kitchen-facilities designers and building contractors, peace of mind that is furthered by continued innovation in ease of installation, features such as quick-disconnect valves. The confidence in Dormont to provide safety from the dangers of gas and being able to rely on Dormont to meet the complexities of building codes are valued emotions. Thus, those in commercial kitchen construction feel a strong emotional connection to the familiar Blue Hose.

As Dormont anticipated competition from overseas and desired to grow its business beyond its current core, the company sought to better understand its emotional connection to its customers and strengthen its differentiating aspects. Even in a product part as seemingly impersonal and commoditized as a gas-utility connector, emotion matters. By using the methods discussed in this book, Dormont gained insight into why they have succeeded so well. In a sea of knockoffs and potentially poorer quality products from competitors, Dormont's customers feel content that the company takes care of them, happy to count on Dormont to provide products that fulfill and go beyond construction regulations and performance requirements.

An emotion-based analysis of Dormont also highlights where the company can focus new attention, where there is the potential to further increase their emotional connection with current and future customers. Dormont's products were routine and common, despite the fact that the product stood out due to its unusual color. The company wanted their products to be more cutting-edge and distinct, to remove the impression of commoditization and to differentiate it from new entrant competitors.

In general, the company wanted their customers to be passionate about Dormont, its products, and their relationship with the company, to feel em-

FIGURE 5.3 ■ Illustration of Dormont's "Blue Hose" gas-utility connector installed.

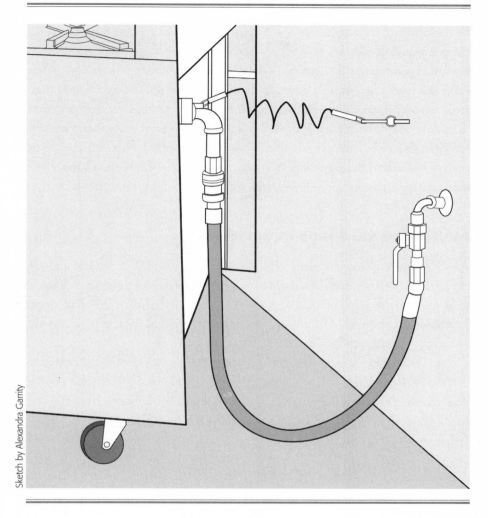

Sketch by Alexandra Garrity

powered by choosing the Dormont brand. In "going beyond the blue" and developing new products that leveraged the emotion of the Blue Hose brand, the analysis of emotion led to emphasizing that Dormont's customers would feel trusted by their own customers for choosing Dormont. They could be confident that, in choosing Dormont's products, they would feel enthusiastic about innovations and their personal relationship with the company, empowered to include the best in their own products and environments, and ahead of the game for choosing state-of-the-art available parts.

The Dormont example illustrates the power of emotion in the purely functional and B-to-B world. While a gas hose seems like a trivial part that will be forgotten after installation, it is really an emotional relationship between a company and a customer base which was so valuable that it led to the acquisition of the company in 2005 by Watts Water Technology for $95M. After carefully studying a variety of business products including physical products such as forklifts and gas detectors, services such as package delivery and product development consulting, as well as software products such as engineering CAD tools and business spreadsheets, we found the Dormont situation to be the typical case: Leading businesses value emotional deliverables in much the same way that consumers value emotion.

Supported Emotions in Services

At the product strategy level and even in the process to design products, physical products and services are no different. What is different between a physical product and a service is that the physical product is tangible while a service is intangible. At the level of execution, services differ from physical products in the same way that one product is different from another.

At the strategy level where business opportunities are identified, there is no real difference in the process of approaching a physical product versus a service. The point is that all of the methods and tools, and all the lessons from the case studies in *Built to Love* apply to both physical products and services.

One exciting service area is that of specialty retail stores. Consider the emotion of shopping at Nordstrom, possibly the most well-known company for customer service excellence. The retail environment is inviting, with an array of high-quality, beautifully presented items. But the service is what you probably remember most. Knowledgeable salespeople greet you professionally and engage you in a way that makes you feel special and important. If you go there often you may have a personal shopper who takes care of you, calls you when something you like comes in, and has already picked out several outfits for you to try on when she knows you are visiting that day.

Nordstrom's service is the people who work there, and who make you feel special and well taken care of—special enough that you want to return for another luxurious experience. Nordstrom sells goods, but the high-emotion service is critical to the overall experience they are delivering.

FIGURE 5.4 ■ Nordstrom's entryway begins the inviting experience.

Photo by Alexandra Garrity

The Emotion of Education

A different type of service that we know well as university professors is that of university education. Comparisons of a university with business and industry are difficult. The financial and reward model for universities is unique, quite different than other business models. Especially at research-based universities, prime capital is top research professors.

At Carnegie Mellon, like many other top research universities, quality education at both the undergraduate and graduate levels is critical to the personal reward that faculty feel and receive. However, classroom education is only part of their job function. Professors make decisions on curriculum changes, degree requirements, and university policies. Professors advise graduate research students who are pursuing their own advanced degree, collaborating with those students on research that leads to publications—hopefully in the top-tier journals—which are reviewed by faculty peers. Faculty members write grants to government organizations and industry seeking funds to pay for those graduate students and support their independent research efforts. Faculty are involved in committees within the university and at national and international levels, advancing common platforms for education, research, and government policy.

As Jared Cohon, President of Carnegie Mellon, points out, "In a university, the principal asset is intellectual capital; the people are the place, and they include some of the most highly charged minds and personalities on the planet. Intellectual excitement is everywhere, along with audacious aspirations to change the future in profound ways. Here we have the intersection of emotions with deep knowledge, creativity, technology, and an exceptional understanding (because we research it all the time) of how these elements fit together in society, its lifestyles, environments, and possibilities."

Taking Carnegie Mellon as an example, the students choose to be at that university. They choose to engage in traditional and radical approaches to education. They choose to buy and use the "product." Their education includes classroom lectures; cutting-edge research projects where they uncover the unknown and set the stage for the future; residential life where they transition from child to adult; and collaborative experiences and social interactions where they belong to and transform a community.

Carnegie Mellon President Cohon says, "The university community is an electrified interchange where, unlike the office or shop floor setting of a manu-

FIGURE 5.5 ■ Carnegie Mellon University, a high-emotion, innovative, education and research environment.

Photo by Ying Lee

facturing company, the consumers are also the producers and where no product or practice is ever regarded as completed, perfected, immune from change or re-placement or complete re-imagining. That's what we do."

Within a university, emotions must be supported; they must be authentic to be sustained. Any product of the university, whether in art, science, technology, social, economic, or medical markets, must be energized by emotional drive if it is ever to travel the difficult path to commercialization or other fulfillment for its ultimate beneficiaries.

The desirability of any university is very much based on emotion. When se-lecting a university, how prospective students feel when they visit, and how stu-dents currently at the university communicate their own feelings and reactions to the university environment have as much sway as its reputation. The reputa-tion comes from the quality of the faculty who also commit to the university, in part for their own emotional rewards. Costs increase when students are treated as individuals; education cannot be commoditized through economies of scale and business efficiency. The effect further promotes emotional connection and outreach.

The sustained emotion spills out beyond the university in both time and space, carried on by alumni who are the outcome, the legacy, and an additional facet of the reputation of the educational service. It even spills beyond its present and past students; through knowledge creation, the university comprehensively impacts and influences individuals and society as a whole.

Unlike most products that are purchased and used, at a university customers are asked to continue to pay for the product long after they graduate. The financial structure of the university is dependent in part on its alumni being committed and giving to the university. Cohon points out that long-term commitment from alumni is inextricably related to how students experienced their universities, how much they are emotionally engaged. Having experienced education as a force in their own personal growth, they understand its power to improve society at large. Nostalgia for one's college days and all that they meant in personal development, as well as pride in the institution, are powerful motivations for recommending the university and for giving to sustain its growth. In practice, supported emotions engendered by students' experience at the university will remain after they graduate.

A university, a specialty store, and service providers in areas as vast as package delivery, IT and database suppliers, telecommunications, and consulting all require emotion-based product strategies that are authentic, providing supported emotions that deliver on their promises. Services are often based on relationships that are developed and maintained over time. Customers can always choose with whom they do business; business is sustained and grows when customers receive emotional fulfillment in their relationship with the service provider. In any product, supported emotions deliver long-term commitments from customers.

Supporting the Value Proposition

Built to Love is about the emotion of products. When a product evokes desirable emotions in a customer, that customer is engaged and excited, finding greater value in the experience of using and interacting with the product. This is the fundamental goal of all companies, for ultimately this is the only enduring way to achieve all the other objectives: greater profit margins, higher customer satisfaction, customer loyalty, and positive word-of-mouth.

Built to Love emphasizes supported emotions in particular, partly because supported emotions are less familiar to companies than associated emotions, even though they offer so much potential. Further, supported emotions are built directly into the product, being the most efficient means to provide emotions. Supported emotions are not supplementary but integral to the product, part of the value proposition.

The buyer of a BMW gets not just acceleration and cornering but also the thrill of the acceleration and cornering. The pleasure of that thrill should be part of the value proposition of the vehicle. "We are creators of joy," says Jack Pitney, Vice President of Marketing for BMW of North America. "All of our efforts in engineering, design, and technology are about one thing, which is creating moments of joy."[15]

When emotions are part of the product value proposition, emotions become answers to needs in the same way that tangible features fulfill needs: deliberately planned and designed in the same way that tangible features are deliberately planned and designed. Companies are much more likely to succeed at developing brands with supported emotions if they follow an effective process to develop the product, one which meets both the functional and emotional desires of their target market.

Putting it into practice—how to be deliberate in designing emotions—is the topic of Chapter 6.

CHAPTER **6**

Product Emotion Strategy

If emotion provides a better return on investment (ROI), how do you create high-emotion products that will realize that ROI? In Chapters 1–5 we discussed the importance and power of product emotions. In Chapter 6 we turn to *how* to design a product emotion strategy for your firm or for one of your product lines, a strategy to consistently deliver a valued and differentiated set of emotions.

The goal is to create products that are different from the competition yet consistent within the current and future product family of your brand or company. A product emotion strategy allows company leadership to be proactive rather than reactive, to be forward looking, to decide how the company should evolve, and to specify and guide what the company should be known for in terms of its products.

Rather than introduce a new product development process, our approach is to inform companies how to adapt current processes to address design that is driven by emotions. In the Introduction of *Built to Love* we introduced our Model of Creating Products that Captivate Customers. The model is shown again in Figure 6.1.

The model has three steps:

1. Determine appropriate emotions for the product's customers. In this step, you determine which emotions resonate with the customer and the company. The customer must want the product and the emotions it arouses, and the strategy must fit the goals of the company. The aim is to create a product emotion strategy from which one or more products can be designed. In this chapter we introduce the eMap as a means to identify appropriate emotions and to understand their respective level of importance for the strategy. In using the eMap to uncover appropriate emotions, we remind you again that your product may be physical, software, a service, or a brand;

FIGURE 6.1 ■ Model of Creating Products that Captivate Customers.

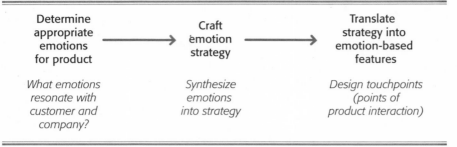

your product may also represent a set or family of products, rather than an individual product.

2. Craft a product emotion strategy from the emotions identified in step 1. The strategy must be concise and specific to the product area of the company, but general enough to enable multiple current and future product solutions. How to craft such a strategy will also be discussed in this chapter.

3. Translate the product emotion strategy into features that realize the strategy. Specific features where the customer interacts with the product—called touchpoints—will deliver the strategy to the customer. Chapter 7 will discuss touchpoints and how to develop them.

This chapter addresses the first two steps. We introduce the elements that underlie any product emotion strategy for product development: the product emotion categories. Next, we show how those categories are made specific for a given product strategy through specific emotions. Finally, we craft the product emotion strategy.

The ideas are driven home through three varied case studies: the Navistar case study from which the LoneStar truck was derived, a small engineering software startup, and a growing robotics company.

Product Emotion Categories

The basic idea is that there are specific categories of emotions that are relevant to product development. Because there are a vast number of emotions relevant to products and their development, meaningful and unique categories can make the consideration of emotions practical, as long as the number of categories is balanced. It should be a small enough set to be usable and cognitively differentiated, and a large enough set to accommodate the complexity of human desires.

A company can use the emotion categories as a foundation for any new venture, building up from that foundation into particular attributes of a brand, physical product, service, software product, or suite of products. In our work we not only use these categories in the context of product development, but we also use the method described in this chapter to determine the emotion strategy for the company itself. Put differently, this method may be used to define a brand in a way that can be clearly conveyed by the emotions delivered by the brand's products.

Based on research studies across multiple academic areas we have identified over 130 terms that describe emotional responses to products, from *excited* and *hopeful* to *indifferent* and *worried*. This may seem like a large number, but people can feel a range of varied and subtly changing emotions in an instant, more than there are words to describe them. If the goal were to label every emotion felt by humanity, 130 descriptors is too few. However, for the practical goal of designing a product emotion strategy, that number is too large for any individual to sort through and consider.

As it turns out, many emotions are similar to one another and may be grouped together. For example, *secure* is similar to *steady*, *assured*, *safe*, and *invulnerable*. By analyzing the similarity of emotions that are relevant to product usage, we derived natural categories, where each category is comprised of emotions that are similar in meaning to one another but different from the emotions in other categories. Our analysis yielded 16 categories—*product emotion categories*—which encompass the emotions that people seek to fulfill with products.

In general, people seek out products that make them feel good, that get their tasks done easier or faster, and improve their personal well-being and attitude. For the most part, people seek positive experiences over negative ones, to feel contented instead of discontented or envious, optimistic instead of depressed and hopeless, passionate and engaged rather than apathetic, proud rather than embarrassed.

The core categories we identified encompass the set of positive emotions that customers seek to feel through products. Table 6.1 lists the 16 product emotion categories, listing positive emotions and their basic definitions. The contrasting negative emotions, such as *embarrassed* in contrast to *proud*, are set in parenthesis, as these are emotions that in most cases a company would want to avoid.

Even in contexts where negative emotions seem to be valued, such as the rebelliousness of teens, there typically will be underlying positive emotional motivators. For example, teens who relish the negative emotions associated with rebelliousness may actually be seeking to enjoy the positive emotional feeling of independence from parental constraints.

TABLE 6.1 ■ The product emotion categories.

This product makes me feel . . .

■ *Independent*: freedom from constraints, feeling of self-sufficiency (as opposed to Reliant)

■ *Secure*: feeling safe, low anxiety, assurance (as opposed to Vulnerable)

■ *Confident*: self-assuredness (as opposed to Uncertain)

■ *Powerful*: feeling of control (as opposed to Incapable)

■ *Passionate*: engaged, fascinated, enthusiastic (as opposed to Apathetic)

■ *Compassionate*: sympathetic, nurturing (as opposed to Neglectful)

■ *Content*: satisfied, at peace (as opposed to Envious)

■ *Optimistic*: positive outlook towards future, all will be OK (as opposed to Depressed)

■ *Joyful*: elation, vigor, a good mood (as opposed to Sad)

■ *Proud*: feeling of effectiveness, of competence (as opposed to Embarrassed)

■ *Sensuous*: arousal, stimulation through one or more senses (as opposed to Undesirable)

■ *Adventurous*: curious, desire for variety, surprise (as opposed to Routine)

■ *Honorable*: trust, believability, wholesomeness, fulfilling norms of righteousness, honesty (as opposed to Inconsiderate)

■ *Luxurious*: feeling of being well cared for, comforting (as opposed to Sparse)

■ *Connected*: feeling of belonging, being included and accepted (as opposed to Lonely)

■ *Distinct*: feeling unique, distinguished, differentiated (as opposed to Common)

By contrasting the positive emotions with negative ones, the positive-negative pairs of emotions set up a *semantic differential* for product emotions. In 1957, Osgood, Suci, and Tannenbaum introduced the science behind semantic differential in the psychology literature.[16] The basic idea is that opposing terms form a measurable scale of meaning upon which humans can differentiate and discriminate. The terms we have identified are contrasting emotions, appropriate as a platform upon which to build a product emotion strategy.

Crafting a Product Emotion Strategy

Every product evokes a unique set of product emotions when used by a customer. Although a specific set of emotions can be crafted for a given product, companies often seek to craft a product emotion strategy: a concise and organized set of emotions that are evoked in a customer when interacting with the product or product family. The product emotion strategy that results from this method may be used to develop an individual product, a suite of products, or a larger brand.

Just as nucleotides are the building blocks of the DNA strands that determine the unique identities of every living thing, product emotion categories are the building blocks of a product emotion strategy. Because the emotion strategy should evoke those emotions that are desirable to persons who interact with the product, the design of the strategy requires a deep understanding of the customer's goals, incentives, and emotional desires.

Once that understanding is derived, the product emotion strategy can be effectively crafted. The strategy needs to be developed such that every attribute of your product connects deeply to your customer's needs and desires, in sync with their core emotions.

The design of product emotions is different from mimicking or capturing the entirety of emotions that a potential customer might feel in their various activities. The entire array of emotions that customers feel is vast, and many of those emotions are not relevant to their interaction with your product. Rather than meeting all their desires, the goal is to connect deeply to those emotions that are specifically relevant to your product.

Many inside a company think they know their customers, especially salespeople whose job description requires this. Salespeople typically do know aspects of their customers extremely well. These are the details they have been trained to recognize as important, such as what each customer typically orders and how each customer will be using each part or service requested. However, the salesperson may know the functional reasons why customers order products without ever considering the emotional deliverables that are desired as well. Such emotional deliverables may connect short-term and long-term with customers.

Understanding the customer is not just the job of sales. Every member of the design team in the largest and smallest companies could benefit by spending more time in the trenches, understanding the needs and wants of their customers, studying both functional and emotional desires. It is that deep understanding that gives insights into both large and small critical aspects of the company and the customer's experience with the products that it sells.

We typically value and use what we can measure. A variety of methods can be used to assess people's emotional desires. People may simply be asked to describe what they are feeling (self-explicated surveys). Trained professionals may observe people to elicit and infer their emotions (ethnography). Scans of people's brains by fMRI machines can be employed to note where the resulting patterns of blood flow indicate intensity of emotion. Each of these methods of assessing and measuring emotions has been shown to be successful in various contexts.[17]

Assessing emotions is a critical market research task, essential for all that follows in developing a product. Yet this is an initial step, for there is more to crafting an emotion strategy than identifying the emotional needs of a target population. A successful company would never develop a new product based solely on focus group opinions, as those opinions must be balanced with the constraints of business processes as well as the context of company objectives, skills, and capabilities.

Similarly, a product emotion strategy involves more than answering current customer emotional desires. The company has internal customers (employees), an existing brand identity and corporate culture, and existing competitors with their own unique attributes, all of which should be accounted for in the product emotion strategy.

Company leadership must use their understanding of their customers and other stakeholders to be proactive rather than reactive, to be forward looking, to decide how the company should evolve as it matures, to specify and guide the company to what the company should be known for, and what cultural values it wants to emphasize and embrace.

Built to Love points out the powerful influence of product emotions on customers and on their views of a company, underscoring the importance of being genuine, of delivering on emotional claims through supported emotions. To make a statement of a product emotion strategy, the company commits to make it a reality and deliver on the promise. To truly deliver on a promise that captivates customers is to deliver on emotions, allowing the right emotions to flow through and energize your market.

A Planning Tool: The eMap

In his book *Emotional Design*,[18] Don Norman discusses the interaction of emotion and product performance at cognitive and visceral levels, finding that products affect emotion through the appearance, use, and satisfaction that people obtain from their use. The question remains how to target and design for specific emotions.

The eMap tool introduced in this section uses the product emotion categories to enable the designer to proactively tap into specific emotions appropriate to the customer and to bring about those emotions through a product emotion strategy that is realized via product features—aesthetic, functional, and otherwise.

FIGURE 6.2 ■ The eMap (emotion strategy map). A version of this eMap chart is available at the end of this chapter for your copying and use.

	−3	−2	−1	0	1	2	3		Attributes
Reliant								Independent	
Vulnerable								Secure	
Uncertain								Confident	
Incapable								Powerful	
Apathetic								Passionate	
Neglectful								Compassionate	
Envious								Content	
Depressed								Optimistic	
Sad								Joyful	
Embarrassed								Proud	
Undesirable								Sensuous	
Routine								Adventurous	
Inconsiderate								Honorable	
Sparse								Luxurious	
Lonely								Connected	
Common								Distinct	

To convert the product emotion categories into a meaningful emotion strategy, we developed the eMap (an emotion strategy map). The eMap is an assessment tool to guide the design and development of the product emotion strategy. It helps a company to understand what customers think of the company and its products today, what they think of the competition, and what emotions they desire from a company and its products. The eMap allows corporate leadership to be deliberate about decisions on which aspects of the emotion strategy will drive future product development. The tool is concrete and actionable, yielding specific emotion attributes that build off its product emotion categories. These specific attributes connect emotionally with the customer and form the basis for the resulting product emotion strategy.

The eMap shown in Figure 6.2 sets the 16 positive emotion terms on the right and the contrasting terms on the left, endpoints on a seven-point Likert scale. In the rightmost column, appropriate attributes are related to each relevant emotion category term. As will be illustrated with our case studies, the eMap allows a company to set a strategy that targets specific emotion attributes to deliver, and also allows the company to assess emotions delivered by the competition. The result is a strategic qualitative tool to help the development team understand what emotional attributes the company must achieve to meet market desires.

There are five steps to using the eMap to organize, process, and synthesize the emotion strategy laid out in the Five Steps to Craft a Product Emotion Strategy (Figure 6.3). Steps 1–4 complete the first step in the Model of Creating Products that Captivate Customers (Figure 6.1), to determine appropriate emotions for a product or suite of products. Step 5 completes the second step: to craft a product emotion strategy.

To understand this process better, we now apply the Five Steps to Craft a Product Emotion Strategy to develop product emotion strategies for a variety of companies, defining or rejuvenating their brand to project it into future product development efforts.

International Truck: Redefining a Brand through Emotion

The LoneStar truck was introduced in Chapter 1. LoneStar is a product of a rejuvenated brand for Navistar's International Truck brand, which was molded as a result of an analysis of its product emotions. Navistar's International Truck brand's roots date back 175 years to when inventor Cyrus McCormick started McCormick Harvesting Machine Company. The company's heritage is agricultural, with McCormick's heirs and William Deering forming International Harvester in 1902.

International Harvester's first trucks, produced in 1907, were designed to serve the farming industry. Over the next several decades, International Harvester grew into a global powerhouse and was one of the original Dow Jones companies. In 1985, after a debilitating showdown with the union, the company faced severe financial problems, sold off the agriculture side of the business, and formed Navistar International Corporation with a principal business in trucking. The company refocused its brand name to Navistar Corporation, and maintained the International brand in its truck division.

FIGURE 6.3 ■ Five Steps to Craft a Product Emotion Strategy.

1. **Define terms** What are the definitions for each product emotion category? Do they differ from the generic definitions of Table 6.1?
2. **Current state** What is the baseline competition or the current state of your own product or brand? Which categories of emotions are relevant and how do they rate today on the 7-point qualitative scale across the positive to negative range?
3. **Goal state** Realistically, based on customer desires and your capabilities, where would you like your company to score on each relevant category? Your corporate capabilities and skills can change; does the eMap say they should?
4. **Attributes** What terms would describe your company's goals for each relevant emotion category?
5. **Synthesis** Which of the resulting attributes are most important, exciting, relevant? Can any be merged? How can they be organized? The result is a concise statement of the product emotion strategy.

Navistar Corporation is a holding company for some of North America's leading transportation brands, operating in three principal segments: vehicles, engines, and services. The International Truck brand has products that compete primarily in specific segments of trucking, the "class 4" through "class 8" segments. These classes represent the weights of trucks, where higher classes are heavier trucks. Classes 4–6 are medium-duty trucks such as beverage delivery trucks, while class 8 trucks include the well-known long-haul "eighteen-wheelers." When beginning their analysis of their brand, International held the dominant market share in classes 6 and 7.

Even before using the eMap to analyze its brand identity, managers at Navistar already recognized the goal: to make customer needs and desires its central focus. They were already carefully managing numerous customer interactions throughout the organization, such as with dealers or financial services during the purchase phase, or with parts and service in the ownership phase.

Even so, there seemed to be much more potential in the brand. This brand had been extremely powerful until the last two decades of the 20th century. Multiple branding studies in the latter part of the century showed Navistar's International Truck brand was not only viewed as earnest and honorable with solid Midwestern values, but also as "dull and boring" like a pair of "old brown shoes" or a "Sloppy Joe!" However, a renewed spirit of innovative designs in some of their new and established product lines began to reinvigorate the International Truck brand.

Senior management recognized that International had a timely opportunity to carefully analyze the brand and to craft an appropriate brand strategy for the new century. The results of an eMap analysis, coming off the initiation of some exciting new projects, impacted the subsequent messaging and product launch of the ProStar long-haul truck, and set the stage for the development of LoneStar and other forthcoming products.

The vision for the new International was to make the brand emotionally exciting, to maximize value of the emotion strategy for the brand. An initial analysis of the customer emotional assessment of the brand, coupled with an extensive analysis of emotional perception about the competition, revealed an opportunity to reach out to current customers and define a new and rich product emotion strategy.

Figure 6.4 shows the eMap for International's goals concerning the emotions its customers will feel when it rejuvenates its brand. As with each of the case studies in this chapter, only portions of the Five Steps to Craft a Product Emotion Strategy are shown due to confidentiality; in this case, the assessment of the competitive landscape is withheld. In the map, G represents the desired goal level, the results of step 3 of the process.

The firm planned to maximize most of the emotions, a strong recognition by the company of the importance of product emotions to its customers. The results of step 4, which makes the tool so effective because it makes the results concrete and applicable, are shown in the rightmost column. These emotional descriptors are specific to International. *Independence* for a trucker is the open road, the cowboy imagery of a Wild West without fences. But even the cowboy had to trust his steed, and the trucker wants a similar feeling of *security*, a reliable truck and trucking company that makes him feel stable. These kinds of descriptive terms turn the abstract and universally applicable product emotion categories into a usable plan for a specific brand.

The final step of the Five Steps is to encapsulate the resulting set of rich multifaceted emotion descriptors into a concise, unified structure that appropriately portrays the emotion strategy of the International brand. Continuums are useful for brand identities in that they define a space where the brands operate and live. Once the space is defined, management can provide points of emphasis in that

FIGURE 6.4 ■ eMap for Navistar's International Truck brand; **G** represents the emotional goal state.

	−3	−2	−1	0	1	2	3		Attributes
Reliant							G	Independent	open road, freedom, cowboy
Vulnerable							G	Secure	reliable, stable, feels safe
Uncertain							G	Confident	**bold**, sense of self, **assuredness** (faith in the leap), the right choice, dependable, quality, **confident**
Incapable						G		Powerful	in control, tough, authoritative, high performance
Apathetic							G	Passionate	**spirited**, passionate
Neglectful				G				Compassionate	supportive
Envious							G	Content	**capable**
Depressed							G	Optimistic	positive, **optimistic**
Sad				G				Joyful	enhancing
Embarrassed							G	Proud	**unapologetic, proud, professional**
Undesirable							G	Sensuous	**sexy, provocative**, eye catching
Routine							G	Adventurous	**challenges convention**, edginess, maverick, trailblazer
Inconsiderate							G	Honorable	**delivers**, trustworthy, honest, **honorable**
Sparse				G				Luxurious	premium
Lonely				G				Connected	accessible, approachable
Common							G	Distinct	cachet, **intriguing**, distinctive, **unique**

space for new initiatives. The goal is to use as few dimensions as possible but keep the resulting message rich enough to drive critical aspects of the company's interaction with its stakeholders, giving structure and definition to the space for the brand. By using the eMap, the structure can be based on the brand's emotion.

For International, the key brand descriptors (shown in bold in Figure 6.4) were mapped on an Emotion Attribute Continuum between two fundamental

FIGURE 6.5 ■ Emotion Attribute Continuum for the International Truck brand.

FOUNDATIONAL								PROVOCATIVE
Honorable	Assuredness	Professional	Unapologetic	Confident	Unique	Spirited	Challenges	Provocative
Proud	Sense of self	Capable	Optimistic			Bold	convention	Sexy
		Delivers						Intriguing

terms: foundational and provocative (shown in Figure 6.5). The continuum for International recognizes that its brand should retain its stability by remaining connected to its history as one of the oldest companies in America.

At the same time, the continuum acknowledges that its brand must be provocative, reaching deep into the emotion of the customer and pushing the edge of what is expected in the industry, intriguing customers with bold products, features, technologies, and services that reset expectations. All products will be foundational, but only some will be provocative.

For example, the standard workhorse long-haul truck—the ProStar—is honorable, proud, professional, capable, and optimistic. It delivers both function and important yet passive emotions, but it was not designed to be provocative. Other new International Trucks are not only foundational in their ability to deliver, but challenge convention in their exterior and interior design.

It is not that every product or service developed by the company must encompass this entire continuum. The goal is to consistently return to the company's product emotion strategy, although each product may fulfill those goals differently. The range laid out in the figure is the basis from which new initiatives can be driven; in general, the set of products (physical and service) should together evoke the entire range of emotions on the continuum.

Understanding International's strategy, spanning the continuum from foundational to provocative, explains why the company was able to develop LoneStar (described in detail in Chapter 1). Recall that long-haul trucks in general are business tools and as such tend to be spartan, designed to minimize weight and maximize efficiency. At the same time that truck and fleet owners seek tools for business efficiency, drivers also desire to be proud rather than embarrassed, to feel reasonably comfortable rather than not, to feel professional in a truck designed for them rather than an insignificant person in a generic truck. It had become clear that the professional, lifestyle-savvy driver needed a professional, lifestyle-savvy truck. To deliver on that opportunity was to be a provocative company that challenged the conventions of trucking.

In 2008, Navistar introduced the LoneStar truck in the International brand with a new look, new features, and a new lifestyle-conscious interior. LoneStar is a product that embodies the whole gamut of the foundation-to-provocative continuum of emotions. The truck is a pragmatic, honorable, and thoughtful business tool. But it also is provocative, sexy, intriguing, and it challenges the convention of what a truck must be in the industry. LoneStar communicates the identity of the company. Designed not only to be a truck, the product is a tangible, strong statement of the brand of the company.

DesignAdvance Systems— Emotions for a Software Startup

DesignAdvance Systems was founded to create engineering synthesis software, to be used primarily by Printed Circuit Board (PCB) designers and electrical engineers. The PCB is that thin board (often green) inside your computer, cell phone, and any other "smart" device. It is the PCB that holds and connects all the CPUs, resistors, capacitors, diodes, and more.

Most engineering software for PCBs assists the engineer in visualization, analysis, and manufacturing once the basic design is known. Few software tools help the engineer or designer in the actual creation process of the PCB. Instead, the layout designer literally clicks and drags upwards of 15,000 components or more onto a PCB floor plan, placing the components where they need to go in the design. This process can take six weeks or longer, impeding time to market. DesignAdvance filled the gap by developing a software design tool, CircuitSpace, which semi-automates the placement of components onto a PCB, reducing initial placement down to minutes. The company's customer base soon included Fortune 100 companies.

Although DesignAdvance developed additional products as it moved from startup status to established company to eventual acquisition, management recognized that the company needed more than a portfolio of software tools. Management took seriously the need to articulate and maintain a product and brand strategy to address product emotions as well, associating the company with innovation, synthesis, efficiency, and effectiveness.

FIGURE 6.6 ■ eMap for DesignAdvance Systems; **G** represents the desired emotional goal state.

	−3	−2	−1	0	1	2	3		Attributes
Reliant					**G**			Independent	*functional, more effective, less reliant on others, escape rigidity of structure*
Vulnerable					**G**			Secure	*stability, reliability*
Uncertain						**G**		Confident	**empowerment**, *successful, high achievement*
Incapable					**G**			Powerful	*efficient,* **control**, *delivers,* **intelligent, smart, enabling, powerful**
Apathetic						**G**		Passionate	*can't live without it, enthusiastic*
Neglectful				NA				Compassionate	
Envious				NA				Content	
Depressed					**G**			Optimistic	*can-do attitude*
Sad				NA				Joyful	
Embarrassed				NA				Proud	
Undesirable				NA				Sensuous	
Routine				NA				Adventurous	
Inconsiderate				NA				Honorable	
Sparse				NA				Luxurious	
Lonely						**G**		Connected	*connected,* **collaborative**, *concurrent, team oriented*
Common						**G**		Distinct	*value added, different,* **distinct, unique**

The eMap tool (see Figure 6.6) helped DesignAdvance articulate the emotions it wanted its customers to associate with the company: *Customers should feel smart, enabled, powerful, collaborative, and distinct.* Considering the issue of feeling smart, without CircuitSpace many of the tasks of the PCB designer are mundane and repetitive tasks that "dumb down" the position of the PCB designer. Those tasks result in the PCB designer's desire to feel smart.

As a startup with innovative products and no direct competition, the company was less concerned with its history and more concerned with its own emotion goal states. Though there were several stakeholders, as new products addressed engineering output, the target customer discussed here is the engineering manager (who also makes the purchasing decision).

The eMap analysis of the relationship between DesignAdvance, its products, and the engineering manager customer led to eight core emotions and numerous emotional attributes. These were the primary ones that resonated with management (highlighted in bold in Figure 6.6). The company-specific emotion terms were synthesized into five key terms that, together, led to the final product emotion strategy statement.

The result was that customers who felt smart, enabled, powerful, collaborative, and distinct led to a strong association of improved productivity with DesignAdvance tools and improved tool adoption, resulting in increased value of the company.

After obtaining the results of the eMap analysis, the management team at DesignAdvance resonated with the outcome. Prior to the emotion strategy analysis, they had not been able to clearly and succinctly state the emotion of its customers with regards to the company. The resulting product emotion strategy statement changed corporate messaging toward the emotion of intelligence of the PCB designer. This was echoed by target users in response to their feelings of success in using DesignAdvance products.

The strategy started driving the development of several new innovations in an industry that had seen little development or new capability in well over a decade; it was also part of the motivation for the company to be acquired by EMA Design Automation. Of all the companies discussed in *Built to Love*, DesignAdvance was the smallest, with fewer than a dozen employees presale.

RedZone Robotics— The Excitement of Dangerous, Dirty, and Dull

RedZone Robotics, another small but growing company (65 employees at the time of this writing), began their quest to commercialize robot technology in the arena of sewer repair. Sewers are dangerous, dirty, and dull environments, ripe for robotic application. A lucrative niche of deep sewer inspection and mapping became a focus of the company.

Because those sewers are so deep and hard to get to—150 feet underground and serving as the city's main sewer lines—the only way to inspect them was

FIGURE 6.7 ■ The RedZone Responder robot may not look pretty, but it carries the emotion that transforms the dirty, dangerous, and dull.

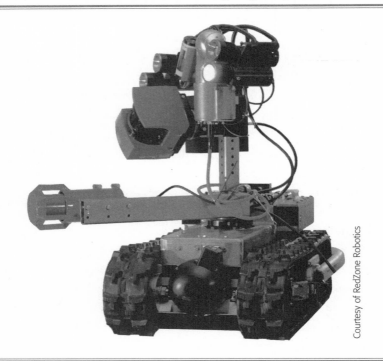

Courtesy of RedZone Robotics

to shut off a portion of the city's sewer system or send a diver down into 5-foot diameter pipes filled with sewage. Sounds fun, huh? Cities often didn't know what was down there. RedZone's Responder robot (see Figure 6.7) succeeded in showing municipalities where the problem sewage blockage areas were: discovering everything from sediment buildup to shopping carts that found their way down a manhole.

The company recognized that their core expertise was in mapping out hard-to-navigate areas. As they sought to expand their sewer business, and move into new areas of wastewater management for application of their mapping tools, RedZone wanted to understand its current emotion state and target a strategic goal state for current and new customers.

Even with RedZone's success, potential customers were hesitant to change their paradigm. Although the company had primarily moved to a service model of taking their robots into sewers and delivering detailed maps, they found new customer acquisitions to be the primary challenge. Those who were not yet customers did not fully grasp enough of the benefits of using RedZone to move out of their comfort zone of status quo. Those who were already customers, however, experienced the results firsthand for their own work sites and tasks, and they were thrilled with the power of the new information that the mapping service provided. RedZone recognized the importance of understanding the emotions of current customers as well as the emotions of potential customers, emotions that the company needed to facilitate new customer acquisition.

Applying the eMap tool separately to potential and current customers allowed management to break apart customers' before-purchase and after-purchase emotions toward RedZone (see Figure 6.8). In this eMap, three states are assessed: the current state of a customer's emotions towards RedZone (C), the state of a potential customer prior to engagement with the company (P), and the goal state desired by management based on their assessment of current and potential customer desires (G).

The two groups of current and potential customers posed a set of dichotomies for RedZone. For potential customers, the newness and adventure of using a robot was attractive, creating excitement that helped RedZone get in the door to make a sales pitch; but once they became customers they did not want adventure but a robust, dependable solution.

Potential customers wanted to avoid luxury that could be seen as a waste of resources, so RedZone needed to avoid any feeling of being a premium or prestigious service. Yet current customers highly valued the comprehensive service provided by RedZone, which went beyond what other companies delivered in terms of the rich information and documentation that streamlined paperwork, verification, and reporting. Customers wanted the luxury of being taken care of in their job task.

Potential customers feared the uncertainty of using a new technology, while for current customers the only uncertainty was what might happen if sewer sediment built up. Potential customers wanted to look smart, but they didn't want to take the risk of anything going wrong.

Analysis of potential and current customer emotions led RedZone to establish its goals for relevant product emotion categories. It may seem surprising that passion and luxury were set to be such strong goals, until realizing that the attributes of these emotion categories really meant "well cared for" with "cutting-edge" service and technology. The customer needed to feel smart about making the choice and thus proud, secure, and honorable for choosing the RedZone service.

FIGURE 6.8 ■ eMap for RedZone Robotics; **C** is Current state, **P** is state Prior to engagement with company, and state **G** is Goal state.

	−3	−2	−1	0	1	2	3		Attributes
Reliant			P		C	G		Independent	*validated*, enabled, expressive
Vulnerable		P				C	G	Secure	**secure**, guaranteed, **no risk**
Uncertain			P		C	G		Confident	self assured, equipped
Incapable					C	PG		Powerful	**insightful**, enabling, in control
Apathetic				P	C		G	Passionate	**cutting edge**, enthusiastic, passionate
Neglectful				NA				Compassionate	
Envious		P				CG		Content	**fulfilled**, predictable
Depressed				C	G	P		Optimistic	engaged, interested
Sad				NA				Joyful	
Embarrassed				C	P		G	Proud	distinction, quality, results oriented, **thought leader**, high end
Undesirable				NA				Sensuous	
Routine			G		P	C		Adventurous	consistent, same
Inconsiderate						CP	G	Honorable	honorable, promise keeping, transparent, defensible, **justified**
Sparse					CP		G	Luxurious	**well cared for**, stands up to scrutiny, comprehensive, meets expectations
Lonely					P	CG		Connected	sharing, **connected**, networked, in touch
Common			G			P	C	Distinct	meeting conventions/standards, **as good or better than**

At the same time, though potential customers at least initially saw the use of robots as an adventure, RedZone's goal is to be seen as a routine partner that provides necessary and expected information, not a new exploration that may result in a feeling of uncertainty. Here is an example where, strategically, being different and standing apart was undesirable and so the company targeted what we would normally consider the negative emotions of routine and common, versus distinct and adventurous.

RedZone wanted their customers to feel confident in their new information, validated in using RedZone's service, thought leaders for committing to this new paradigm, well cared for by the company, and connected to the company and the new technology and infrastructure that RedZone maintained. The reaction from the sales group was that the emotion strategy was right on, that "this is what we do." The reaction from management was, "This is what we must deliver, what closes the deal; it is foundational, strategic, and long-term."

An Actionable Strategy

The eMap allows companies to gain insight into emotions currently engendered by the company, its brand, and its products, and to develop a strategy for future efforts. Every future product should connect to the emotions of the brand or product family. The design of this connection is not arbitrary, random, or irrational. It is a thoughtful, analytical process that can provide corporate and brand strategy for future product development efforts and customer relationships.

If used right, the eMap is a translator, making the connection between company and customer as a driver for product innovation. Using the eMap takes effort, but the results are actionable insights, useful for molding future company-to-customer transactions.

The first part of *Built to Love* argued that emotion is not simply an extra sales tactic but an opportunity for which products are the answer. Product emotions are the means to earn the fanatical level of customer loyalty desired by every company. The product emotion strategy is the essence of what drives that loyalty, and the eMap gives clear and consistent direction for a strategy to deliver products that deeply resonate with your customer.

Because the emotions need to be individually defined for each target application, the method is general, and is applicable in consumer and B-to-B applications, low-tech and high-tech, physical products, and virtual services. The result is a strategy.

But you can't make money selling your strategy; you make money by selling products. So the last step is to connect the product emotion strategy to product touchpoints: points of interaction with the user's senses. One touchpoint that is quite visible is the product's form: a connection to the sense of sight.

Form follows emotion! That is the subject of Chapter 7.

The eMap

	-3	-2	-1	0	1	2	3		Attributes
Reliant								Independent	
Vulnerable								Secure	
Uncertain								Confident	
Incapable								Powerful	
Apathetic								Passionate	
Neglectful								Compassionate	
Envious								Content	
Depressed								Optimistic	
Sad								Joyful	
Embarrassed								Proud	
Undesirable								Sensuous	
Routine								Adventurous	
Inconsiderate								Honorable	
Sparse								Luxurious	
Lonely								Connected	
Common								Distinct	

CHAPTER 7

The Emotion of Form and Touchpoints to Create It

Sexy sports cars, fierce pickup trucks, bold tools, sleek phones: the visual form of a product exudes emotion. These emotions can be intense and exciting (as with a Ferrari), or they can be the subdued emotions of the comfortable and familiar (as with a Honda). There are no emotionless product forms, for even the idea of *emotionless* evokes repulsive feelings of deadness, fatigue, and dreariness.

A product's visual form is a highly influential source of value to customers, steadily supplying product emotions that are experienced every time a customer looks at, touches, or uses a product. Each and every interaction of the customer with the product is a *touchpoint*, a means to stimulate emotion and implement a product emotion strategy.

Touchpoints are the end result of emotion-based design (or any approach to design). They are the last step in the Model of Creating Products that Captivate Customers (see Figure 6.1 in the previous chapter). There are other ways to create emotion besides visual touchpoints, such as the feel of using a product or of relating to service personnel during a transaction. In Chapter 7, we focus on a product's visual identity as an example of how to evoke product emotions.

Given the power of a product's visual form, company leaders should be aware of and understand how the form of a particular product can be used to fulfill their strategy to provide valued emotions. Design of visual form is an example of efforts invested in every physical product. Money may be spent on a thoughtful and meaningful design that fulfills a product emotion strategy; the same money could be spent on an arbitrary design, without regard to product or company brand.

In a world where every product form evokes emotion, whether planned or unplanned, the design of a product's form should be intentional and calculated as a means to connote specific and desired emotions. The design of the product form should not be random. It should involve thought, research, and a deliberate emotional connection to the customer.

When you see a BMW driving down the road you sense the excitement, luxury, passion, pride, and independence: the emotion of driving and owning a BMW. You feel its emotional essence, whether it's a 750 sedan, a Z4 roadster, an X6 sports activity coupe, or any other vehicle in its product line. BMW has succeeded in making its products both recognizable and consistent in style, along with the emotions that style connotes. BMW products share a family resemblance that is distinct from competitors, a distinct visual identity.

The distinctiveness of visual identity for a product and its family may be analyzed and broken down into its constituent parts. For BMW, note the low, broad stance, the double, rounded, rectangular grill with the vertical lines, the headlights moving out in perspective. The visual identity, for BMW or any product, is a powerful way to evoke valued emotions in customers—by connecting to the brand's emotion strategy.

What is potentially so powerful, and often missing from unsuccessful products, is an alignment of the visual identity and the product emotion strategy. The process of creating successful forms comes from translating the product emotion strategy into a visual form language in the product. That language provides the basis for a family of products to work in unison, communicating the emotion of the brand.

From Harley-Davidson to Harley Earl

Emotion of a Harley

For family resemblance to be effective, for starters, the products must be recognized as belonging to the brand. To see how this works, look to one of the most passionate brands of all time: Harley-Davidson. Harley-Davidson motorcycles evoke pure emotion. Passion drives the purchase, maintenance, and social interaction among owners of Harleys. There are many cheaper alternatives, yet people long for and spend significant resources to purchase a Harley. There is even a matchmaking website for Harley owners.

The passion for the company is felt in every bike that the company produces. Figure 7.1 shows several motorcycles. Which one do you think is a Harley? Figure 7.2 is a photo of an actual Harley. Does that help?

The Harley bike is recognizable, from its styling to the sound of its mufflers. The look alone is unique, stimulating emotion within its customer base. The identity of a Harley bike is seen in its V-Twin engine, the teardrop fuel tank (and

FIGURE 7.1 ■ Examples of motorcycles: Which one is a Harley?

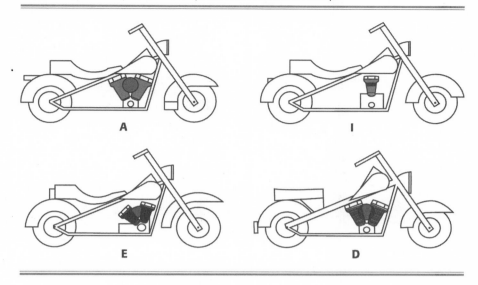

FIGURE 7.2 ■ Harley-Davidson motorcycle.

Photo by Larry Ripple

FIGURE 7.3 ■ Harley features.

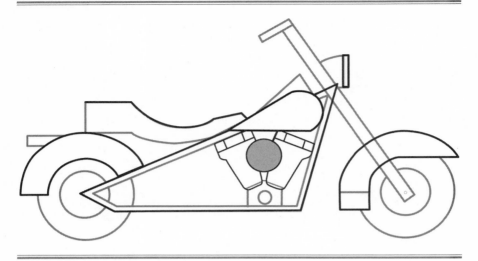

its geometric relation to the V-Twin), the cupped seat, the circular headlight, the triangular frame, and the thick fenders. For you non-Harley riders, can you pick out the Harley in Figure 7.1 now?

To make it easier, Figure 7.3 clearly shows these features. It should be obvious that 7.1(A) is the Harley. What is interesting is that 7.1(D) has some, but not all, of the features; Figures 7.1(I) and 7.1(E) have little resemblance to a true Harley.

We tested the effectiveness of Harley's visual language by generating a selection of motorcycles, some clearly Harleys, some clearly not, and some in between. We then asked Harley owners to pick which ones were Harleys, as we asked you to do in Figure 7.1.[19] We used the line abstractions shown in Figure 7.1, much like the ones designers often use when sketching concepts.

Using that style of representation we expected some divergence, as those not trained to think more abstractly might not catch the subtleties among the designs. Nonetheless, the results were outstanding (see Figure 7.4). Two bikes had all of the core features of a Harley (A and M), three bikes had varying levels of the features (B, D, and S), and the rest had few to no features that make a Harley a Harley. As seen in the figure, the owners, even using abstract line drawings, clearly recognized the two Harleys as such. As the features dropped off, so did the association to Harleys.

Because Harley has a clear and distinct visual identity, the specific emotions of Harley can be uniquely associated with that identity, allowing the products

FIGURE 7.4 ■ Recognition of Harley features by Harley owners; A and M have all the features of Harleys; B, D, and S have some; the remainder have few to none.[20]

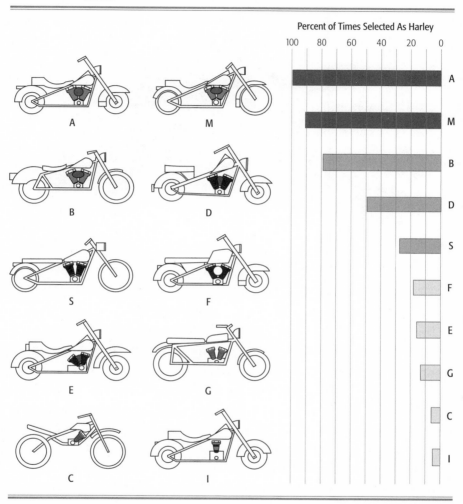

to evoke a consistent set of emotions in customers—feelings of desire, of power, of pride, of independence, of connectedness. The look of the bikes promotes and evokes each of these emotions. So the form of the Harley ends up being a significant and essential tool to deliver these emotions.

In sum, the process is to identify which emotions the products should evoke, namely, the product emotion strategy, and then to specify which form features evoke those emotions via the visual identity.

FIGURE 7.5 ■ The Harley V-Rod.

Photo by Remi Jouan; source: Wikimedia

The visual identity allows the emotions to carry forward into new products, to shape new products to be visually and emotionally consistent with others in its family. In the 1990s, Harley experienced significant competition from Japanese speed-oriented bikes, which younger buyers seemed to prefer. In response, Harley developed their version of the streamlined bike. In doing so, they quickly found themselves challenged by creating a new, liquid-cooled bike (earlier bikes were air-cooled, but the speed and acceleration of the new bike required a more aggressive, liquid-cooling effect).

At the same time, Harley needed to maintain their brand identity—the look and feel of the Harley brand. Significant engineering went into development of a new engine (in partnership with Porsche), a radiator, and an exhaust system that all maintained the look of a Harley. The result was the V-Rod (see Figure 7.5), a competitor to Yamaha and Honda, but with the look, feel, and emotion of a Harley-Davidson.

Emotion of a Buick

Speaking of Harley . . . another Harley who was known for vehicle design was Harley Earl, famed car designer and head of General Motors' styling from 1927 to 1958. Earl is credited with bringing styling and visual brand differentiation to the auto industry at a time when Ford was emphasizing functional designs (in any color the customer wanted, "so long as it's black").

Earl introduced the first concept car (the Buick "Y-job"), tail fins (a 1948 Cadillac design), and the Corvette. As Hollywood special effects created emotion through its 2D visual world, Earl created emotion through the 3D visual world. Earl understood how to elicit special-effects emotion in vehicles because his previous career was creating custom automobile bodies for Hollywood stars. Earl's introduction of clay modeling may have come from understanding quick scene creation.

Buick was one of the car lines whose design Earl oversaw. Although the Buick line predates Earl, the period when Earl was head of design was effectively the beginning of Buick's current brand identity. Features such as the bump atop the grille, side portholes, and the wave-shaped bodyline began under Earl's reign. These features, among others, enabled everyday people to recognize a Buick as different from competing brands such as Ford, and to sense the emotion behind the Buick vehicle: the sensuous curves, the smooth power.

Many of Earl's design features remain in Buicks today, formally incorporated into a "speedform" by recent head of styling Wayne Cherry, as a core form model for future Buick designs. Looking over the history of Buick designs from Harley Earl's 1927 Cadillac LaSalle to Wayne Cherry's concept cars such as the Bengal, there are certain key features that make a Buick a Buick. Most prominent is the grille, an oval shape with the slight bump on the top. There was a second, squarish grille used for many models in the 1960s and 1970s post-Earl: uninteresting and nondistinct. The Buick emblem rests in the center of the grille.

It turns out that there are very few basic shapes that Buick has consistently used for the inner and outer fender as well as for the hood line. Most prominent are Buick's side portholes and its wave-shaped body that starts in the rear and swoops down to the front fender. Within the consistency of these distinctive shapes and their interrelationships is the Buick brand.

Variations on these shapes inspire the variety of different Buick models that can be designed. These shapes may be inferred from studying the history of the products of an established brand, as we did for Harley and Buick. Alternatively, shapes such as these may be intentionally designed as a statement of brand, a proactive stance that can connect the corporate brand and product emotion strategy to product form. This consistency establishes a visual identity that communicates the brand and emotion across existing products as well as those that will be

FIGURE 7.6 ■ Potential Buick designs based on Buick's visual brand language.[21]

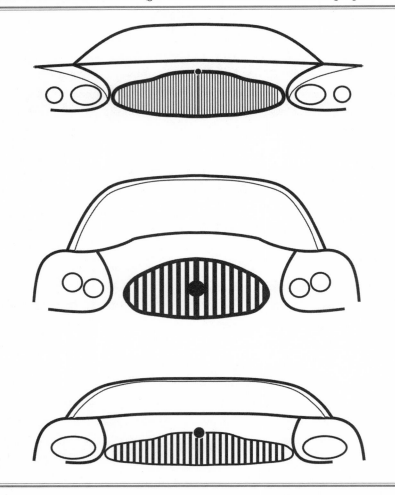

designed in the future. Once identified, these shapes allow anyone to create their own distinctive product, in this case a Buick (such as those in Figure 7.6).

Loss of the consistency of these basic shapes (the constraints that define the basic Buick relationships) would eliminate the family resemblance that facilitates brand identification, disrupting the ability for the products to evoke the emotions already associated with the brand. That is why some more recent vehicles such as Buick's Lacrosse look generic, because they have lost Buick's differentiat-

FIGURE 7.7 ■ A contemporary Buick that has moved away from the traditional grille identity.

Photo by IFCAR; source Wikimedia

ing visual features. Buicks have historically had a slight bump on the top of the oval, but some recent Lacrosse grills have no bump (see Figure 7.7). They are just an oval that looks much like the Ford oval.

Understanding the visual brand language—the visual form language that captures a brand—allows for consistent identification of a brand over time and differentiation from the competition. The visual brand language can also provide the basis for trade dress and other intellectual property protection of the form identity.

For new companies, a visual identity can be strategically designed and thoughtfully planned, providing a means to communicate the company's product emotion strategy. Some new companies are so focused on getting a functional product to market that they miss this powerful, long-term opportunity.

For established companies with an inconsistent past, identifying the historical visual language for a company is an opportunity to choose those features from the past that best connote the product emotion strategy of the company, today and tomorrow. As new designs are brought forward, those features can be strategically and consistently maintained. Such consistency and thoughtfulness can connect with the best features of the company's past and set the stage for a new future, using the power of visual identity to communicate a new direction for the company itself.

Integrated Brand Identity Map

One company that built on the power of visual identity as it moved into the future is Navistar, whose turnaround is symbolized and embodied in the LoneStar truck discussed throughout *Built to Love*. Chapter 6 described customers at the turn of the 21st century who saw Navistar's International brand as being like "an old pair of brown shoes," comfortable and well used but unexciting. The styling of the trucks was equally uninteresting.

An analysis of the form of over 2000 International trucks from the 1920s to 2000 revealed eighteen different eras of vehicle design.[22] The lack of consistency was indicative of the variation in design without regard to a core visual identity over the history. Some of the designs were exciting, and others plain or nondifferentiated. Chief Designer Dave Allendorph set out to create a consistent, contemporary, and forward-looking design theme for International trucks, a look to "challenge convention."

To draw upon International's long and strong heritage, Allendorph identified four of the eighteen earlier eras that connected to International's product emotion strategy (see Chapter 6 for the derivation of the strategy). Building on those four eras, two additional contemporary themes, and his own insights and vision, Allendorph created several forms that communicated International's product emotion strategy and provided a form basis for future designs.

The base design is the cab for the workhorse long-haul truck, the ProStar (see Figure 7.8, top). This cab style is used for several other day cabs as well. A foundational vehicle promoting honorable, proud, professional, optimistic, and confident emotions, the ProStar embodies the recognition that International "delivers."

Other Navistar vehicles, even if different in style, must maintain all of those emotions; *any* truck that Navistar produces under the International brand must be foundational in the emotions it delivers. But the LoneStar goes further, pushing the product emotion strategy to the provocative level: to be sexy, intriguing, spirited, and bold.

The LoneStar (see Figure 7.8, bottom) challenges convention and makes a strong emotional statement of "work hard, live well," both inside and out. Its bold style connects back to the earlier eras of the 1930s but has a contemporary look and feel that balances fuel efficiency with the stance of a classic design. Its strong chrome retro grille, confident chrome bumper, vertical oval headlights, bold 3D curves, and chrome air tanks introduce a unique and bold design that will command attention on the road. That boldness gives way to comfort and

FIGURE 7.8 ■ Navistar's International Truck examples: ProStar (top) and LoneStar (bottom).

Photos courtesy of Navistar

caring for the driver in the interior, where social features and sleeping spaces work in synergy.

To deliberately evoke a consistent set of emotions through the form of the product, it is important to foster recognition of the product line and to connect the product emotion strategy to the visual identity. An Integrated Brand Identity Map is one approach to this connection between emotions and physical form. The Map sets visual identity designs along the rows versus the product emotion strategy along the columns. The Map indicates which attributes of the product emotion strategy are found in the visual designs. The Integrated Brand Identity Map for International is shown in Figure 7.9.

The core visual language, the six key visual eras identified by Allendorph as key to future International truck styles (two contemporary, four historical), appear along the rows. The product emotion strategy, organized across the continuum from foundational to provocative (as discussed in Chapter 6), rests along the top.

In the Map, each visual form is meant to drive future form designs at International and can be related to each product emotion strategy attribute. Although every company is different, many will have certain foundational emotions that all of their products should evoke. In the Map, those are best placed to the left. Toward the right are those emotions that are still core to the company but may not be part of every product.

The top of the International Map is the Emotion Attribute Continuum (shown in Figure 6.5 in the previous chapter). The darkness of the lines across the rows indicates which of the emotions that shape connotes. As may be seen, the ProStar form (second row) is foundational but not provocative, while the LoneStar form (top row) includes all the attributes of International's product emotion strategy.

Visual Brand Language

All the examples in this chapter so far have been for vehicles, but vehicles are not the only product class where form language matters. Every product that is carefully designed should have a consistent theme that promotes the emotion of the brand.

If you look around your house you can recognize a variety of products that you connect to their brands. Think about durable goods like washers, dryers, and stoves, and the associated brands. Three of them—KitchenAid, Whirlpool, and Maytag—are all owned and designed by Whirlpool Corporation. Yet

FIGURE 7.9 ■ International Truck's Integrated Brand Identity Map.[23]

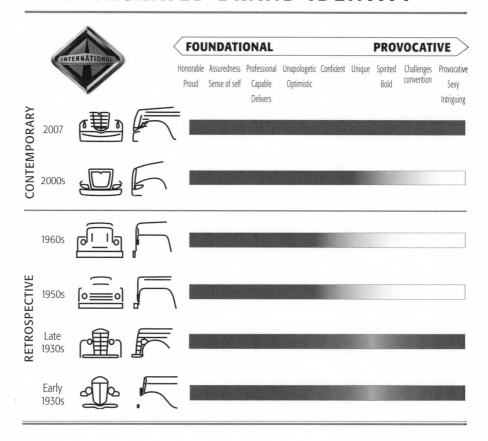

INTERNATIONAL'S INTEGRATED BRAND IDENTITY

each looks distinct, carrying its own brand identity. Whirlpool Corporation has worked diligently to define a separate visual brand language for each of their brands. These visual identities are distinct from each other and also from the competition. Because every form connotes different sets of emotions, each brand from Whirlpool Corporation conjures up different emotions in its customers.

Consider the difference between the Whirlpool and KitchenAid brands. According to Whirlpool Corporation, the Whirlpool brand customer values simplicity and effectiveness, saving time and effort. These goals result in targeted emotions of confidence, a sense of energy, being active and alive. On the other hand, KitchenAid customers value relationships, sharing experiences with family and friends, the joy of cooking with quality they can feel. This results in a different set of emotions, those of friendliness, honesty, authenticity, purpose, and a sense of robustness and craftsmanship.

These are two different types of people seeking the same functional products: a range, an oven, a dishwasher, or a refrigerator. The parent Whirlpool Corporation does not make two entirely separate ranges or refrigerators. The core functional product is generally the same. What varies are the interfaces, the details, and the colors. These surface features give the products in the two different brands a different feel.

Whirlpool Corporation seeks consistency within a brand through a consistent look, and consistent emotions communicated through the brand's products. Under the tutelage of Chuck Jones, VP of Global Design, Whirlpool Corporation has created a template for the themes of the different brands through visual brand languages. Whirlpool creates form languages that, when assembled into a product, create the look, feel, and emotion of the brands. The curves and proportions are mapped onto the features of the products—the handles, knobs, and overall shape of the refrigerators, dishwashers, ovens, and more. The geometric curves embody the essence of the product forms.

Visual brand language, when consistent, can provide a basis for intellectual property (IP) protection. In Whirlpool's case, they are aggressive in filing design patents to protect the look and feel of their handles and grips, surface detailing, and user interfaces. The core set of curves is a trade secret, but their logos are trademarked and the text-based aspects of the user interface are copyrighted.

Whirlpool goes beyond form language to include colors, materials, and finishes to complete the brand language, and protects these aspects of their visual brand language through trade secrets. Figure 7.10 summarizes Whirlpool Corporation's approach to their visual brand language. This result is a unified brand message and long-term equity through strategic IP protection.

When a visual brand language is applied, the same functional product looks and feels quite different. Figure 7.11 shows a Whirlpool brand and KitchenAid brand double oven. Though they look quite different, their functional guts are essentially the same. The figure shows how the visual brand language changes the expression of the product. If you look at other products from the two brands, they look like part of the respective families.

The distinction between the identities of the Whirlpool and KitchenAid brands have led the brands to different product lines as well. KitchenAid is well

FIGURE 7.10 ■ Whirlpool Corporation's approach to visual brand language.

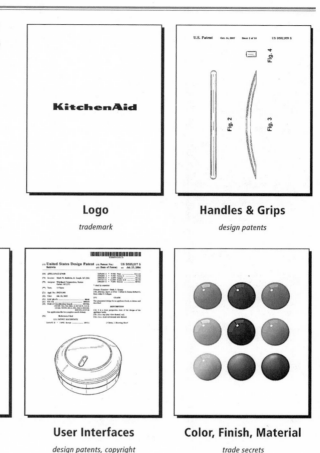

Courtesy of Whirlpool

Logo

trademark

Handles & Grips

design patents

Surface Detailing

design patents

User Interfaces

design patents, copyright

Color, Finish, Material

trade secrets

known for countertop appliances like blenders and mixers, carrying the experiential joy of cooking into an arena beyond kitchen-based durable goods. On the other hand, Whirlpool's focus is on saving time and effort, which moves that brand to produce other types of durable goods, like washing machines and dryers. KitchenAid doesn't make washers and dryers; Whirlpool doesn't make mixers and blenders. Their product lines are consistent with their family emotion strategies.

As seen in these case studies, the design of the product form should not be haphazard. It should be the outcome of deliberate planning and design, resulting in clear and distinct communication of the company or brand's product emotion strategy. Any good designer, whether consciously or through gestalt impression, uses a visual form language for the products that they create. Designers

FIGURE 7.11 ■ Comparison between Whirlpool and KitchenAid brand double-oven styles.

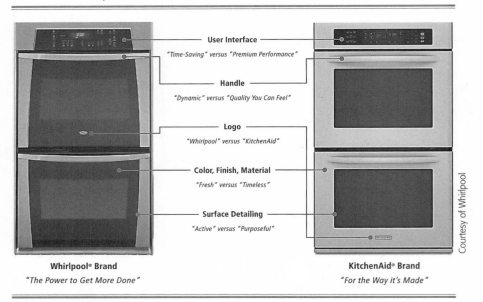

User Interface
"Time-Saving" versus "Premium Performance"

Handle
"Dynamic" versus "Quality You Can Feel"

Logo
"Whirlpool" versus "KitchenAid"

Color, Finish, Material
"Fresh" versus "Timeless"

Surface Detailing
"Active" versus "Purposeful"

Whirlpool® Brand
"The Power to Get More Done"

KitchenAid® Brand
"For the Way it's Made"

Courtesy of Whirlpool

often start with a theme and use that theme throughout the conceptualization process. The redesigned 1998 VW Beetle, for example, was designed based on a simple half-circle; the half-circle is seen on the roofline, the wheel wells, and more. Such themes may be seen in products all around you.

The goal is always to connect the visual form language with the product emotion strategy, a process we will soon discuss.

Buildings Talk: The Language of Architecture

Architecture is one notable area where the language of the product—buildings—can be clearly connected to product emotions. Buildings engage us emotionally, for after any new building is created, critics and laypeople debate opinions, project the aesthetic meaning of the building, and revisit the building's implications as history evolves.

William Mitchell, Director of the Design Laboratory and Professor of Architecture and Media Arts and Sciences at MIT, points out, "While we may look at a picture for seconds or minutes, experience a movie that lasts an hour or two, or read a novel over a few days, we may inhabit buildings for months, years, or lifetimes. Our individual experiences of architecture are complex, and

FIGURE 7.12 ■ The Apple store on Fifth Avenue in New York creates an emotional first impression.

Photo by Andrew Cagan

are often constructed over extended periods of time, so our emotional responses are correspondingly diverse, multilayered, and evolving."

Mitchell describes the power of emotion in buildings. At the outset, we respond to first impressions of buildings, initially as we walk or drive up to them, and then as we enter and view the interiors. These first impressions are instantaneous—like first impressions of people—and they establish a background against which later responses develop.

The Apple flagship store on New York's Fifth Avenue is an example of a building that creates a powerful first impression by presenting a breathtakingly transparent glass cube and a prominent Apple logo directed towards the street. The architecture provides the delights of cool, elegant minimalism and draws those outside into a bustling, product-filled retail space that invites the customer to examine and buy (see Figure 7.12).

William Mitchell also states that a building can evoke emotion by visually resembling some other thing that we recognize: "The concrete Parthenon in Centennial Park, Nashville, for example, closely resembles the original, marble Parthenon on the Acropolis in Athens. In doing so, it brings to mind the glories of classical antiquity, and associates these with the 'Athens of the South.' American Collegiate Gothic college campuses, which refer us to the traditions of their venerable predecessors in Europe, pursue similar strategies." So do themed restaurants, retail spaces, and hotels.

Mitchell says that a building can take the form of an abstract diagram that, by virtue of structural similarity rather than immediately recognizable resemblance to something, serves as a metaphor: "Grand, solid masonry bank buildings, prominently located on Main Streets, reassuringly represent (whether truthfully or not) the solidity, permanence, and civic importance of the businesses they house. And the curved titanium forms of Frank Gehry's Bilbao Guggenheim have become a widely understood metaphor for the economic and cultural rebirth of that Spanish rust-belt city."

In architecture, a visual attribute of something can stand for the thing itself (called *metonymy*). Steel is strong; to reassuringly express strength, an architect may therefore expose the steel frame of a skyscraper. Roofs are sheltering, so to express the idea that a house cozily shelters a family, an architect may give it a particularly prominent roof. The showiness of McMansions expresses the wealth of their inhabitants.

In architecture, a part of something can also be a visual cue for the whole (called *synecdoche*). Architects use natural materials such as wood and stone—fragments extracted from natural settings—when they want to bring nature to mind. Similarly, they use steel, glass, concrete, and plastic when they want to position buildings in our minds as elements of the system of industrial modernism. The lobbies of many companies will boast some symbol of the roots of the company, or a projection of what the company wants to be.

Powerful works of architecture are memorable; mediocre ones are forgettable. The planned construction of a new building presents an opportunity to a company. Rather than constructing the new building as a place that communicates ordinariness, or creating the new lobby as simply a place to sit, the new space can be a symbol of the company's product emotion strategy. Through its visual language a building can communicate and create emotional value for the customer. Architecture has the potential to be an expression of the corporate brand and corporate

FIGURE 7.13 ■ Steps to Translate Emotion to Touchpoint Features.

1. Identify touchpoint attributes that would engender each emotion:
   a. Based on other products used by target market;
   b. Based on previous experience and training.
2. Integrate into product design features.
3. Test product with target market to see if product engenders emotion:
   a. Obtain feedback.
4. Iterate until product effectively engenders emotions.

principles. It can be a window into what the customer can expect of their experiences with the company.

The building can be truly *built* to love!

Translating Emotions into Features

The product emotion strategy leads to touchpoints. The design of the touchpoints themselves requires a focused approach by discipline. Engineers must create technology to deliver the emotions. Programmers must code applets and platforms. Chemists must deliver compounds as pharmaceuticals, or as appropriate flavorings or smells.

Industrial designers must deliver visual identities that engender targeted emotions when customers look at and use a physical product. Interestingly, industrial designers are trained to create product forms that people react to, but engineers, chemists, and programmers often are not attuned to the emotional reaction of their end users. Nonetheless, they each have the skill-set to accomplish this task.

Figure 7.13 summarizes the Steps to Translate Emotion to Touchpoint Features. To deliver visual touchpoints, the designer must consider each emotion and the characteristics of lines and surfaces that might engender the set of emotions. Often, designers will look to other product types that a target market uses and identify those form features that will resonate with the targeted set of emotions.

The designer of an electric vehicle might look at contemporary products used by environmentally aware people, such as compact fluorescents, or high-tech products such as smartphones, or cutting-edge but environmentally sound fashion items. The prominent lines of the forms might be carried over into the current design, bringing emotions along.

Forms might also be associated with other experiences and insights that the designer has gained from past designs or insights projected forward. After iteratively exploring design forms that might reflect the desired emotions, the design is tested against potential customers. Positive and negative feedback will propel a new iteration of design changes and lead to the next round of feedback.

This approach of feedback and interaction is used in visual design and the same approach is used in all aspects of product development that seek out customer-driven products. In their book *Creating Breakthrough Products*,[24] Cagan and Vogel recommend at least three iterations of design exploration and feedback to converge on the best design.

The best design will be one that engenders the desired emotions.

Shape Grammars and Computation

Although designers are trained to create forms that elicit emotions, firms would benefit if they employed a more formal approach to doing so. If nothing else, those of us who are nondesigners could understand why different features were included in the design. This becomes especially important as engineering takes a product to production. Here, changes to the form—for example, to cut manufacturing costs—can have a profound impact on the resulting emotions that customers feel.

One example is seen in the design of the Pontiac Aztek, a disaster of a vehicle for the first decade of the new century. To sum up its design, *Car and Driver* in 2000 referred to its "rather cartoonish, space-cadet styling" that "does not include a personal disguise for when you're driving in crowded areas."[25] In sum, it was ugly! Rumor has it that within an early month following its initial release, *one* car was sold in the entire country of Canada!

Whether the rumor is true or not, the point is well taken (and we wouldn't be surprised if it were true). There were few to no positive emotions engendered by this design. Interestingly, a concept version of the car looked far more appropriate, aggressive in styling but more coherent as a whole. There was clearly a mismatch between design and production.

It turns out that there is a formal approach to understanding, representing, and using visual product languages known as "shape grammars." George Stiny, a mathematician architect originally at UCLA and then at MIT, invented shape grammars in the 1970s. Although developed in the world of architecture, Stiny's method brought rigor and consistency to more traditional product development as well.

You may remember the concept of "expert systems," popular in the 1980s. Expert systems used sequences of rules of knowledge stored in the computer to formulate logical answers to a query. In shape grammars, Stiny also created a production (or rule-based) system that works not with words, but with shapes. Each rule allows a transformation of an emerging design toward a final completed design. It has been shown that you can break a visual identity into discrete chunks and a sequence of rules that will generate the design of a product.

Shape grammars were used to generate the Harley-Davidson features shown earlier in this chapter; shape grammars were also used as the basis for analysis of the Buick brand.[26] Shape grammars are versatile, having been composed for certain classes of cars, for coffee-maker brands, and even for Chinese-styled chairs. Extensive use of shape grammars in architecture has captured buildings in the style of Frank Lloyd Wright, Palladio, and more.[27] Unlike their distant expert systems cousins, shape grammars can be more like fractals, logical in the details but sometimes seemingly illogical and creative in developing an overall product design.

With today's computer technology, formal shape grammars can be implemented by computers to allow efficient and automated exploration of many different variations of a design. Computers can use a shape grammar that models a particular brand to generate thousands of designs, each of which fulfills the brand identity defined by the visual brand language. The important question then becomes which design will yield high sales volumes and appeal most to the marketplace.

By merging marketing research methods, statistical data mining, and artificial intelligence, shape grammars have been implemented and used to test different product design attributes with the customer, providing an alternative to traditional focus groups. Product designs are experimentally altered, and market research participants state their preference for the products that they are shown. The computerized system learns what individual customers or customer segments visually prefer, and is able to iteratively generate new product designs to match their preferences.

Figure 7.14 shows the output of one such new market research tool applied to the design of SUVs, exploring the appeal of the product to customer segments interested in buying an SUV. Images were shown to customer segments in a market research experiment, and participants reported their preferences for the SUV designs. Based on their reported preferences, the system mapped out their product form preferences by customer segment.

In the upper right are contours for a customer segment found to prefer an SUV with lower ground clearance and a larger grille, while the contours in the lower left show the preferences of a different customer segment, one that prefers a vehicle with higher ground clearance, large headlights, and a smaller grille. Shape grammars allow the computer to generate product images, even images of nonexistent but viable products, speeding up and adding precision to market research for product aesthetics and appeal.

This market research tool allows computers to help interdisciplinary product development and marketing teams to more efficiently and accurately develop products with product emotions. Designers can explore new form ideas and know that they are within the visual brand language. Engineers and management can clearly understand and maintain that brand identity. Marketers can then test the different concepts against a target market in a quick and controlled environment to uncover which designs engender targeted emotions and which ones people like. These powerful new marketing research and design tools provide insight into what proportions and relationships people prefer in the form of the product while maintaining the brand identity and product emotion strategy of the company.[28]

Visual Closure

Throughout this chapter, we demonstrated how a product user's emotions could be stimulated by the product aesthetics. However, if you walk away from this book thinking that you just need to make your company's products look good in addition to working well, you've missed the point. The value we describe lies deeper than "skin deep."

Especially in modern times, aesthetics are valued because of the emotions that they evoke, not because they are simply pleasant to the senses. The term *aesthetics*, introduced by Baumgarten in 1750–1758 in his book *Aesthetica*, signifies the science of sensory knowledge. Aesthetics has since become a major branch of philosophy. Even earlier Greek philosophers such as Plato believed that Beauty stimulates feelings of pleasure and that Beauty represents "the real value of life."[29]

FIGURE 7.14 ■ Appeal of vehicle shapes to two market segments.[30]

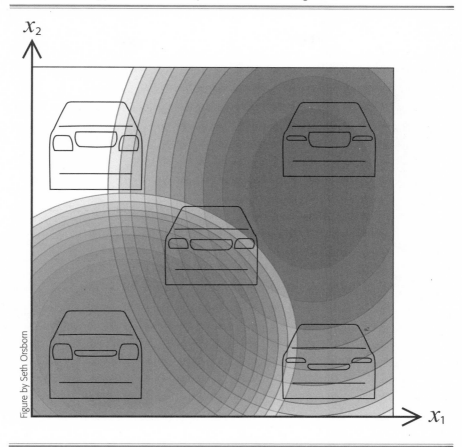

Figure by Seth Orsborn

In our current postmodern era, aesthetics continue to be valued for their emotional enjoyment.[31] In the same way that philosophers have consistently believed that aesthetics are an avenue to the emotions that people desire to feel, the end goal when creating product aesthetics is to create valued emotions, not merely to make products that look cool or relevant.

In sum, visual form is a critical part of communicating your brand and the emotion generated by any product. Visual form languages are powerful tools to proactively translate the product emotion strategy into product form. Visual forms offer an opportunity to consistently and clearly provide valued product emotions that resonate with your customers.

Chapter 7 focused on form because of its power in evoking emotions and because aesthetics and visual design sometimes feels like a black art to many. As we've shown, it is not a black art at all. The same deliberate and analytical planning for any other product touchpoint—any interaction of the customer with the product—can and should be pursued.

For a physical product, other aspects should be addressed in similar fashion, features such as materials and colors. There are other touchpoints for all products; in fact, every product touchpoint has the potential to provide emotion. Touchpoints are the means to transform a product from mundane to exciting, from ordinary to emotionally satisfying. In vehicles, the feel of acceleration can be ordinary or extraordinary, evoking feelings of fuel efficiency or of power. Touchpoints can be found in touchscreens and other user interfaces, acoustics and sounds, flavors and tastes, motions and vibrations. Product form is an example intended to illustrate a path for the design of all touchpoints that can deliver the emotions you want your products to evoke.

CHAPTER **8**

Meeting Societal Needs:
Positive Roles for Emotion

Emotion is fundamental to all that is human, a fact that people recognize, appreciate, and enjoy. Sights, sounds, and surfaces stimulate us through touchpoints; there is no engaging product or activity that does not evoke some aspect of our emotions. Although we all understand that we are emotional beings, what has been poorly understood to date is the extent of the opportunity companies have to provide emotions in products.

Product development as a field has concentrated on how to create products that are of high quality, with desirable functional attributes and characteristics. The nonfunctional part of product development—emotional benefits—often has been seen as some kind of black art, the serendipitous outcome of creativity and luck. Yet emotion not only stimulates initial purchases, it also brings customers back for re-purchase. Emotion creates the loyalty firms strive to achieve for long-term growth.

Emotions are also profitable, increasing sales volume and the ability to price for higher margins. Emotion sells, yet because of uncertainty about how to create products that resonate with customers at an emotional level, many firms focus their innovation efforts exclusively on what they already know how to do well: maximize the performance or functional aspects of a product.

The critical next step for businesses to understand is exactly how to create products that engender specific emotions. To enable the leadership of your company to envision how emotion applies to your firm, in Chapters 8 and 9 we look at the reach of emotion through multiple examples of how a variety of firms and organizations have met emotion-based opportunities in two contrasting areas relevant to today's marketplace.

The first area, discussed in this chapter, relates to societal issues that include sustainability, health for the aging, social action, and globalization. These are issues that people are clearly emotional about, but how does that translate into product emotions? How will emotion impact and even enable solutions to critical social problems? How different will services be if they are designed to provide emotional value as well as functional value? We discuss a variety of important societal issues that will only be effectively solved if they resonate with the emotional needs of individuals and society as a whole.

Emotion of Sustainability: Trash You Love

Kasey Jarvis is a Creative Footwear Designer at Nike. During a trip to Vietnam he visited a facility where the footwear factories in the region send their waste material to be sorted into enormous piles. Each pile contains different footwear materials: leathers, synthetic leathers, rubber, foams, and textiles. Some of these materials get recycled or repurposed, but much gets buried in landfills or burned as fuel. Seeing the volume of scrap material all in one place was a shocking experience that became the driving force to propel Jarvis to develop the Nike Trash Talk, the world's first performance basketball shoe made from manufacturing waste.

There was an opportunity to significantly reduce those piles of waste, going above and beyond standard waste-reducing efforts. Moreover, there was an opportunity to engage the customer so that they felt like they were *participating* in helping the environment as opposed to just knowing that sustainability is addressed. The Trash Talk shoe invites the consumer to accept waste they can see in a form that is unexpected.

After that trip to Vietnam, over a period of about a year and a half Jarvis and his team learned how to make shoes from waste material. Ground-up bits of rubber scrap became the foundation for the new rubber outsoles. For leathers and synthetic leathers, the larger scraps were sliced into small shapes that could be nested and stitched together for maximum efficiency. Leftover foam chunks were ground down and reformed into new midsoles. Where waste materials couldn't be used, environmentally preferred material (EPM) options were chosen. Shown in Figure 8.1, the Trash Talk was introduced in the spring of 2008.

Part of the challenge was to learn how to manufacture from waste a performance shoe that was just as durable as regular shoes, up to the standards of elite athletes who play primetime on national television. An additional challenge was to make everyone *recognize* that the shoe would perform, to *feel* like the shoe was durable. And it wasn't just wearers who needed to feel that the shoe would hold up; even after attaining the high standards for durability from a manufacturing

FIGURE 8.1 ■ Nike Trash Talk.

Photo courtesy of Nike

standpoint, there were still lurking fears among the team that shoes made from waste couldn't be as durable as regular shoes.

"Emotion in design can be a powerful motivator that builds enthusiasm and drives people to accomplish great things," says Jarvis. "Emotion can also be a paralyzing, fearful barrier that clouds reason and can snowball into an insurmountable barrier."

Fortunately, one of the strongest supporters of this concept was Steve Nash of the Phoenix Suns. Nash is an activist and an athlete who supports the community through childhood education and addressing environmental issues via the Steve Nash Foundation. Like most people, Nash was initially nervous about the idea of wearing basketball shoes from waste material. He wanted to be supportive, but he didn't want the shoes to look like garbage, to have pieces fall off, or to have a shoe blow out while he was playing.

After reassurance and testing the shoes, Nash agreed to wear the shoes in the NBA All-Star Game in early 2008. By doing so, Nash's performance gave internal Nike employees the needed proof to overcome their fears and doubts and the basis to begin the task of addressing the same fears of eventual wearers.

To be a real solution, it must not only be feasible to manufacture and believable through product quality, the product must also result in a viable business.

Jarvis points out, "In order to be honest about the Trash Talk concept, the shoe needed to be mass-produced, made from scrap in large quantities and at a profit, not just a handful of shoes for a one-hit-wonder event. Making shoes from scrap in a production setting means figuring out how to optimize the construction process and come up with solutions that will work long-term."

Assembling shoes from multiple bits and pieces can be potentially time consuming, complex and labor-intensive, each a costly proposal. All of these factors were big sources of fear and presented significant challenges.

Making shoes from scrap material is clearly only a small part of the solution to the problem of waste in footwear manufacturing. According to Jarvis, society's challenge is to use up existing waste while creating less, eventually making products with no waste at all. While the Trash Talk is not a perfect solution, or a long-term solution, it is a real solution to an existing problem. It makes a dent in environmental waste and does so in a way that makes sense for business.

Jarvis states, "People have to be careful not to love an idea to death. Eliminating waste from landfills and keeping garbage out of furnaces is a cause that's easy to get excited about. Naturally, some want to extend the sustainable thinking as far as they can throughout the product and process. After presenting the Trash Talk to a group of designers, I was approached by someone who said he loved the concept, but couldn't understand how we could allow the shoes to be sold in stores where the shelves, floors, and tables were all made with hardwoods. For him, the store we chose wasn't 'green' enough for the message behind the Trash Talk. While the retail channel may not have been a perfect fit from a sustainability standpoint, it was the ideal location for connecting with kids who want to buy basketball shoes. If we had tried to extend the sustainable nature of the Trash Talk all the way through to the retail channel it was sold in, we would have killed it: death by enthusiasm. Instead, we had a balanced approach that brought us one step closer to environmental friendliness while creating a sustainable business. The dual edges of sustainability must work in concert."

When sorting through the complex emotions involved with creating sustainable products, it's easy to get discouraged by all the challenges and contradictions. Looking back, when you have identified a problem and have solved it, you've made real progress that can be measured, transforming initial discouragement into the pride of moving forward. The end goal is zero impact on the environment. As each piece of the system works towards that goal, the system as a whole will result in less waste or emissions.

The starting point, of course, is to identify the opportunity. When you recognize that the opportunity can be emotion-based, emotion is the drive, the challenge, and the reward. Environmentally conscious products provide a valued emotional experience for the customer, and the process and reward of creating those products provides a fulfilling emotional experience for the designers as well.

Every business that manufactures products can likely find ways to reduce the impact of waste, but the greater opportunity for innovation is to create new marketplace demand for the environmentally friendly, creating a rewarding, empowering, and proud professional experience.

The Emotion of an Aging Demographic: Getting Older, Living Well

Emotion-based opportunities can begin with social and cultural developments such as the sustainability movement. They can also be derived in specific target segments, such as Baby Boomers. It has been projected that as Baby Boomers age, current levels of services in general, and healthcare services in particular, will be insufficient to handle the numbers of older adults in the U.S. and across the world.

In the U.S. alone, there are over 78 million Boomers—one quarter of the population. It isn't just that the volume of services is insufficient. According to Craig Vogel, Professor in the School of Design, Architecture, and Planning at the University of Cincinnati, the quality and extent of the services are insufficient to meet the expectations of this particular post-50 generation. Companies are struggling to understand how to meet the expectations of this lucrative and demanding market.

In 2005, Vogel founded the Live Well Collaborative, a joint initiative between the University of Cincinnati, P&G, General Mills, Hill-Rom, and Citi, to understand how to meet the needs and expectations of consumers who are age 50 or older. The collaborative focuses on how to create products that fulfill both functional and emotional desires.

"The quote from Andy of Mayberry, 'Floyd, give me a haircut but don't make it look like a haircut,' epitomizes the expectation of the Boomer," says Vogel. "Implied in Andy Griffith's statement is the simple principle of universal design: Help me to look, feel, and be my best, but do not make it look like I need assistance."

Boomers expect the limitations of aging to be accommodated for but not overtly; solutions can in no way stigmatize these older consumers who are unwilling to sacrifice their optimism, desire for adventure, confidence in their achievements, and passion for life. By taking Boomer emotions into account, there is an opportunity to provide products to those who don't want to feel like they need them.

According to Vogel, health issues in particular will color many of the choices aging people will make in an attempt to live a quality lifestyle of optimism and hope despite declining health. As humans approach the age of 50 they often face multiple challenges. A few fortunate individuals who have managed their health effectively and have a great genetic inheritance will be able to sustain a high quality of life for several decades. Others have the opposite situation and find themselves significantly challenged by health issues that have been handed down to them.

A third category of 50+ consumers lives in denial. They are health time-bombs and will encounter severe limitations, medical interventions, and life-threatening conditions, including diabetes, stroke, and heart attacks.

As couples age, they often face health issues at different times and at different scales. The result is that one partner becomes a home-care provider to the more challenged counterpart. Any variance from the expectation of aging gracefully and healthily will likely cause frustration and emotional distress in the Boomer. The opportunity for providers is to accommodate these emotions while maintaining as positive a lifestyle as possible.

One project developed at the Live Well Collaborative with Hill-Rom, Inc., focused on the emotions of those involved with Alzheimer's disease. One important insight from the effort was that Alzheimer's is not simply the patient's disease; it becomes a partnership between the patient and the caregiver. As the patient becomes less aware of others and of their surroundings, the pressure on the caregiver—usually the husband, wife, or child—increases, creating psychological stress and impacting their own health.

Whether in the role of patient or caregiver, the Boomer does not want to feel the need for assistance. When faced with Alzheimer's, however, the patient-caregiver partnership is pressured with additional responsibilities. As one example, Alzheimer's patients typically take multiple medications throughout the day. Although the task of taking or administering medication sounds simple, a seemingly trivial task for which patients and caregivers would be embarrassed to seek aid, the patient's compliance in taking medications is a major issue for Alzheimer's caregivers.

Live Well developed a service concept of medicine delivery. A week's worth of medicines are delivered to the patient. Each day's medicine is presented on a sheet of paper perforated into strips. The strip is removed, easily ripped open, and the dose is removed from its plastic bubble. The strip of paper also contains the medicine's name and information about it.

What is so interesting about this simple solution is that, early on, the patients can take their own medicine. As their condition deteriorates, the caregiver can take over, using the same easy-to-use method. This service solution indirectly gives the caregivers a sense of support, and reduces their stress and anxiety, allowing them to devote more time to the patient or themselves.

Whether purchasing lifestyle products or services, managing health-related issues, or planning living environments, 50+ consumers expect high-quality design that integrates style and technology without stigma. The good news is that Boomers have more wealth than did previous older generations, and are willing to pay for solutions that work physically and address their core emotional wants.

Emotion of Social Action: The Product of Hope

There are emotion-based opportunities amidst some of society's deepest ills. Of poverty, theft, murder, prostitution, and illegal drug use, which does *not* have an emotional element as a root cause? There is an emotional element to each one of these issues, because most, if not all, social issues have emotion at their core. All of these problems are serious, and comprehensive solutions are either infeasible or unknown.

Positive emotions can be used to begin solving some of these issues, a step toward a more complete solution that benefits society as a whole, and provides unique opportunities to augment any company's brand.

For example, consider Publicolor. Founded in 1995 by Ruth Lande Shuman, Publicolor, a not-for-profit youth development organization, is addressing the growing crisis in the U.S. of underprivileged kids dropping out of school. With 4 million young people out of school and not looking for work (as they feel they lack the basic skills needed to enter the workforce), one in every 100 citizens in prison, and 82 percent of inmates high school dropouts (not to mention, the staggering costs of incarceration), it is no surprise that this is a critical social issue. Publicolor creatively addresses these issues head-on by using the power of color and design and a continuum of youth development programs to creatively engage high-risk students in their education.

They begin with Paint Clubs that empower hard-to-reach students to change the way their schools look and feel by teaching them to paint warm, inviting colors in their cold, colorless school environments. The absence of color is not benign, and vibrant color is the start of school transformation.

Four afternoons a week and every Saturday, underperforming students learn the marketable skill of commercial painting as they paint "energy, hope, and determination in schools where lethargy and hopelessness abound," says Shuman. "Publicolor paints visual clarity in spaces marked by confusion for people whose daily life is often filled with chaos. Publicolor paints a visual journey through color combinations and transitions, thus stimulating the eye and thereby the brain."

This is the beginning of engagement. Publicolor also "paints" dignity and respect in environments used by people who daily experience the indignities of poverty, reflected in the deteriorating environments of the schools.

Because all involved in site transformation develop a new sense of pride and ownership, vandalism goes way down, creating a greater sense of safety for all. With minds no longer frozen by fear, teachers can finally teach and students can finally learn. Teacher attendance improves at Publicolor schools; 83 percent of teachers who were recently surveyed report having higher expectations of Publicolor students after seeing them engage in a school-wide initiative.

These higher expectations are key to better performance. Hope, dignity, pride, respect, and a sense of safety: All of these emotions are highly valued, and lead to behaviors that improve learning and relationships. These emotions begin an upward spiral of positive social change; hope leads to improved expectations and performance, which leads to greater hope.

Publicolor achieves its success through a caring staff who ensure each day that each student experiences a small success—a door well painted, a connection with a tutor, a productive conversation with a role model. As a result, Publicolor students develop the self-confidence needed for the risk-taking that is inherent in real learning.

In 2008, 100 percent of Publicolor's formerly at-risk students graduated from high school in four years versus the norm of 31 percent; 87.5 percent of Publicolor's students went on to college. All are the first in their family to go to college, so they are paired with mentors to ensure that they stay in school and graduate; 92 percent of the Publicolor college students returned to school the next fall versus 65 percent of first-generation students nationwide.

Publicolor builds on its starting point of positive emotions to teach students useful life practices. Shuman explains that Publicolor students learn good work habits and transferable skills: the importance of showing up on time, with a good attitude, of taking initiative, of thinking logically, of constructively giving directions about what to paint and what not to paint, and how to take a big project and break it down into a sequential series of smaller projects. Students learn how to be leaders, not bullies, how to take and give direction, how to be part of a team and work collaboratively, how to take personal and collective responsibility.

Shuman adds, "Publicolor students transform from being hopeless victims to engaged citizens."

Equally important to students' success is the engagement of Publicolor volunteers. Each year, over 2000 corporate volunteers informally mentor these youngsters while painting alongside them every Saturday. Nearly all the students say this is their favorite part of the program. The students love making a difference; and they love meeting people who care enough about them to spend a whole Saturday with them. Volunteers inspire the students to stay in school, graduate, and even pursue a college education.

Shuman points out, "Somehow, life today seems so isolating—most of us have very little free time. We are bombarded with technology; we spend even less time interacting with friends and colleagues, let alone in a meaningful way. Volunteering to paint with Publicolor enables very busy people to slow down, connect with one another and with young people who desperately need to spend time with good role models." The added benefit is that they're helping to improve public school education.

Corporate team-building results in friendlier relations among a company's co-workers and between co-workers and supervisors. All benefit from the pride they feel in their company's efforts to make a difference by supporting youth development organizations like Publicolor.

"No longer does the corporation look like an inhuman, competitive money machine," says Shuman, "It now has a heart." Many end up thinking that if the company can show concern for students, then it can show concern for its employees. This leads to a much greater sense of appreciation and loyalty among employees, along with a desire to do more.

Publicolor's product is multilayered. A service for painting schools, a tutoring system for kids, but really the main product is hope: a positive outlook for people who otherwise see no path to a successful future.

Publicolor is not the only way to invest in the future of society. Social action of any kind, in any country, addresses true issues for others and is emotionally rewarding to those who are helping, whether they are helping in food kitchens or guiding underprivileged children and adults in their education, administering to those in medical need, or giving emotional support to the homeless. If those people whose emotions are boosted work for a company that encourages involvement in that social issue, then the emotions for that company are boosted both by the employees who participate and by the customers who see the heartfelt contribution from the company.

Social action is a means to develop more engaged employees and more engaged customers. Through social action, companies all over the world have an opportunity to energize their brand in a way that resonates with employees and customers alike. Companies have a unique opportunity to lead by example. By being concerned and engaged citizens, they can inspire their employees to truly make this a better world.

Emotion of Globalization: Cultural Design for Local Markets

Thomas Friedman's 1999 book, *The Lexus and the Olive Tree*, captures one issue that companies face in selling their products globally. On one hand, people desire the Lexus: prosperity symbolized through luxury goods. On the other, people wish to maintain their identity and retain the traditions of their heritage: the olive tree.

Friedman connects this struggle to politics, but we can use his insights to highlight the difficulty of taking a product design from Detroit, for example, and attempting to sell it in New Delhi. The company may use a localized advertising campaign and possibly minor aesthetic changes, hoping to create associated emotions without the power of supported emotions that resonate with the customer base. The need is for a truly localized product that is designed with functions needed by the local market and supported emotions that are desirable to that market.

This was the impetus for the creation of the $2500 Tata Motors Nano, an inexpensive car that met the urban needs of Indians at a price and feature point that they demanded. Even for those firms that recognize what a local market needs in terms of product function, there remains the opportunity and challenge to the global company to understand the emotional expectations of each market. Only after understanding the culture and its implications will a company understand how to connect to the emotional desires of that local market.

Xianyang Xin, Associate Professor of Design at Hong Kong Polytechnic University, argues that to meet local market needs and desires a company must understand the uniqueness, appropriateness, and pleasantness of an experience within a culture. Understanding unique cultural behaviors is important in order to develop products that can trigger positive emotional responses from users who are influenced by their unique cultural backgrounds.

Appropriateness—how products properly fit certain social and cultural contexts—is important in maintaining long-term positive emotional connections. Together, uniqueness and appropriateness support a memorably pleasant user experience. That pleasantness promotes customer loyalty and positive word-of-mouth.

One can't force uniqueness, appropriateness, or pleasantness on a group of people, however. Xin describes an interesting example in the classic rice cooker, a home appliance invented in the East. The most important factors contributing to the success of Japanese and Chinese rice cookers are understood through the rice-eating culture of the Far East. Rice is an Asian staple that is emotionally important. When cooking became a time-consuming event in the process of transforming from an agricultural society to an industrial economy, having rice for a meal became difficult for many young independent professionals. Properly cooking rice takes time and requires delicate control of heat at different stages. The rice cooker allowed people to enjoy a home meal with rice and became as essential as the stove.

Automated food preparation in general wasn't what Asian people sought, though. As so nicely captured in the Taiwanese film by Ang Lee, *Eat Drink Man Woman*, cooking and eating is a deep, emotional cultural symbol of the Asian way of life. The rice cooker was accepted as a tool only within the cooking ceremony. When Western companies introduced high-tech, multifunctional, computerized versions that made not just rice but other foods like congee and soup, which were programmed to cook slow or fast with built-in timers, and had layers of nonstick coatings, the high-tech product removed the high-emotion cultural experience, was found confusing and disruptive, was felt to be unsafe, and led to its demise.

FIGURE 8.2 ■ Lotus skincare series for Chinese elderly.

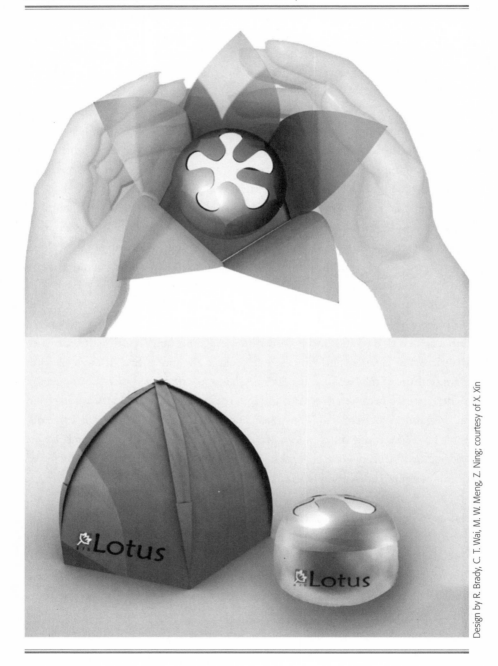

Design by R. Brady, C. T. Wai, M. W. Meng, Z. Ning; courtesy of X. Xin

In contrast to the failure of the high-tech rice cooker, Xin likes to talk about a successful culture-based design developed by students at Hong Kong Polytechnic University in a project sponsored by the P&G IDSA School Collaboration Program. A series of skincare solutions were developed for Chinese elderly, who believe that skin appearance is a reflection of internal health which can be restored and maintained through special ingredients of traditional Chinese medicine rather than unknown Western chemistry. A lotus design was proposed (see Figure 8.2) with different kinds of ingredients targeted for different geographical regions with different skin problems due to the variations of climate conditions. Xin says, "The lotus is an important ingredient used in Chinese medicine and cooking for restoring internal balance of Yin and Yang."

The concept was well received by interviewees for its immediate emotional connection to users through the use of Lotus as a brand name, as the lotus is a symbol of purity, beauty, and love in Asian culture. It also connects to Buddhist beliefs. In Buddhist tradition, the Buddha takes a lotus position while sitting in order to demonstrate absolute solemnity and purity. The package design also reflects the blossom of a lotus flower. Normally, a lotus flower only blossoms for three days. On the first, it opens up just a little then closes; in the early morning of the second day it will be half-open but gradually close again in the afternoon; on early morning of the third day, it will completely open but wither by the afternoon.

Because of this open/close pattern, the lotus is also a symbol of day and night: Yin and Yang. The closed package represents the closing position of the lotus flower; the opened package with cap reflects the opening position of the flower and seeds inside. The skincare design is a well-developed concept that is unique and not copied, appropriate to Chinese culture, and supports a pleasant experience for Chinese elderly.

The philosophy of a culture is akin to the brand of a company. The philosophy provides the context, heritage, and identity of the culture, and the DNA of what aligns with, supports, and imbeds within the culture. The cultural philosophy provides the foundation to build high-emotion experiences that fulfill the market's emotional core.

To design products consistent with the emotion of a culture generally requires more than to copy the style of iconic images. It is to understand the context of the opportunity in terms of current social, economic, and technology factors and also in terms of geography and ideology.[32,33] Cultural-based innovation fulfills the utilitarian and emotional needs of individuals as well as situating personal needs in a social and cultural context through unique, appropriate, and pleasant experiences.

Culture is one of the highest emotional experiences that people connect to, embrace, and defend. Culture-based product opportunities lie in every corner of people's lives, and can be spotted through observations of simple everyday events if seen through a cultural philosophy—a culture's brand.

Product Emotions and Societal Needs

It would seem that taking steps to alleviate societal crises or to help those in need would be successful and appreciated just for providing needed functions, such as education to the disenfranchised or work skills to those in poverty. To achieve greater levels of sustainability by reducing waste might seem to be enough: selling the same products as before but now with green-certified labels. The same cars, shampoos, or other products that have been successful in the U.S., France, or Germany should, in theory, be successful everywhere else, as long as the prices are right. A person dealing with natural ailments as they age should accept any product that improves his or her ability to function, seemingly without wanting more.

Yet public school dropouts need hope in order to invest the needed effort to stay in school. Consumers want to feel like they are participating in sustainability efforts, not just know that a company recognizes and is addressing the problem. Consumers in different cultures seek products that are integrated into their sense of self, not disconnected versions of products found elsewhere. Those who are aging want to maintain their sense of dignity and ability. People are emotional about these and other issues, and emotion can serve as the opportunity and source of effective solutions.

Societal issues, and the emotions that surround them, are important considerations for all companies: those firms whose focus is social welfare as well as those whose interests have historically centered on shareholder welfare. The market today is more attuned to societal issues and more concerned with the impact of those issues. Companies in tune with societal issues directly reflect that in their products and demonstrate how they impact people's lives and environment. Any societal issues of concern to customers will affect the companies they want to do business with. These are all critical reasons to consider the emotions of societal issues in the development of product and brand strategies.

Emotional Reach in Technology Products

Chapter 9 examines the emotion of technology in the domains of nanotechnology, medical products and healthcare, space systems, and robotics. Some if not all of these technologies would be considered by most to be unemotional, removed from that which is human.

Emotion is often contrasted with all that is rational and analytical, as in *logical* arguments versus *emotional* ones, or *analytical* decisions versus *emotional* ones. Technology falls clearly on the side of the objective and rational and may seem like it has nothing to do with anything emotional.

Throughout *Built to Love* we have demonstrated that emotion is critical to the success of all companies, including those selling technology-based products. We will see that even in the most extreme use of technology, product emotions provide value to customers. The following examples illustrate how emotions affect the design of emerging technologies and how emerging technologies affect our emotions.

Unseen and Unknown: From Fear to Comfort of New Technologies

Technology today advances with such rapidity and complexity that, for many, fear initially overtakes hope. Think, for example, of nanotechnology, which is the study of nanometer-scale machines that are one-billionth of a meter in size—about the scale of a molecule or 1000 times smaller than the width of a human hair. Nanotechnology is used today in products for better antibacterial surfaces, lighter and stronger composite materials, and shinier cosmetics, among others. As nanotechnology advances, it will continue to be developed into products used by people in a variety of arenas, including energy, medicine, and electronics.

With all that potential, according to Philip LeDuc, Associate Professor of Mechanical Engineering at Carnegie Mellon University, the ultra-small size makes the nanoscale machines invisible to the human eye. In some cases, this may promote fear of the unknown and unseen. LeDuc notes that books written about nanotechnology have perhaps contributed to a general fear, distrust, and unease with its use. Books such as Michael Crichton's *Prey* describe the potential ability to create nano-machines or nano-viruses with unintended destructive capabilities.

LeDuc points out, "What might be emotionally negative on one size scale, such as fear of unseen technology, may be very different on a large scale, where the nano-scale components are integrated into a larger macro system that integrates into people's lives."

For example, state-of-the-art sporting equipment like tennis racquet frames and skis deliver superior properties using nanoscale particles, resulting in enhanced feelings of power and passion for athletes. Nanoscale inclusions in cosmetics deliver improved shine and longevity, and are used by those seeking the confidence of splendor and the luxurious feeling of wearing new powders. In these and many other cases, the nanotechnology itself may not evoke positive reactions but the final product that results from nanotechnology's capabilities may evoke positive emotional attributes within the consumer.

Thus fear becomes passion and accolades designate nanotechnology as impressive, challenging, surprising, edgy, and even fashionable. In fact, companies such as Apple have used the word *nano* to their advantage in naming surprisingly "small" but powerful products. Interestingly, some components in the electronics technology that we use every day, such as those used in the Nano iPod, actually are produced using nanoscale technology.

One area where nanotechnology may profoundly impact human well-being and emotion is in healthcare. LeDuc's research illustrates the sophistication of future medical technologies, through the development of an implantable "nano-factory" (see Figure 9.1). Current medical treatments for a diversity of diseases, including heart disease and cancer, use drugs that are manufactured in chemical factories before being delivered to patients through mechanisms such as intravenous injections, controlled release, and ingestion.

An implantable nanofactory could potentially create an artificial system at a nanometer-size scale that is able to convert preexisting, deleterious molecules already in the body into beneficial compounds.[34] Additionally, this approach could enable chemical reactions in the body that a person might otherwise be unable to make happen due to their inherent medical conditions.

FIGURE 9.1 ■ Artist rendition of an implantable nanofactory.

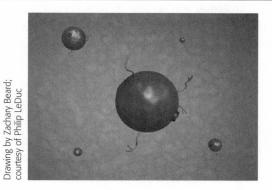

Drawing by Zachary Beard; courtesy of Philip LeDuc

Such a capability could elicit a range of emotions from excitement and the feeling of adventure to the fear of the unknown, because it is occurring inside a person's body. It is therefore essential to both deliver technical capability that improves healthcare and also to create supported emotions of confidence and security due to the technology's effectiveness.

Associated emotions can then be utilized to reinforce those positive emotions through education and communication, relating the nanofactory to macroscale drug delivery that people already connect to, products that already improve or save the lives of millions. Turning the technology into a product that emotionally connects with the patient will be the critical task in a future design.

The healthcare industry has benefited enormously from technology advances, as have those receiving its services and care. Whether it's because of the reassurance of the doctor or the track record of healing those who are ill, society in general accepts medical technology as safe enough, eventually becoming confident and dependent on technology without being swayed by the potential downfalls.

Consider the negative effect of X rays on the body's cells balanced against the advantage of a newly healed broken bone or success in removal of a cancerous tumor revealed in an X-ray film. The healthcare industry puts much of its focus on technology for future improvements.

Robert Schwartz, General Manager of Global Design for GE Healthcare, says that most medical-device companies are effective at creating advanced technologies. In fact, healthcare companies are engaged in what Schwartz calls a "technology arms race," with each company attempting to create faster, quieter, more powerful, more accurate devices and procedures at a lower cost. These companies have been generally thoughtful in terms of patient and operator interaction and usability. Their best products present a strong and authoritative impression in medical professionals and patients alike.

According to Schwartz, the medical procedures we go through are among the most emotional events that we humans may encounter, yet in practice, there often is little emotional support built into diagnostic and treatment experiences or the products that support and enable them. Complex equipment protocols, heavy patient loads at institutions providing diagnostics or treatments, cost pressures, and an emphasis on high-technology as the solution often eclipse needed attention to what can become a journey of anxiety.

Few healthcare companies have begun to explore how to use product emotions to differentiate their products in the marketplace beyond product aesthetics. Fewer companies have focused on how to improve the emotional experience of clinicians and patients.

Yet think about a company that is not your typical healthcare provider: the Mayo Clinic in Rochester, Minnesota. The Mayo is not only widely respected for its team approach to medical diagnosis and treatment, it is also a leader in the development of better medical experiences: from methods to help patients relieve stress during surgery to new physical environments to enable more comforting patient-doctor interactions.

It is ironic that medical technology which is so invasive in human interaction can also be inhuman in its emotional connection. According to Schwartz, companies are beginning to experiment with emotional support techniques, for example, using music, video, ventilation, and lighting to create calming or distracting illusions or effects. As examples, Schwartz refers to certain diagnostic imaging procedures that reduce the sense of confinement or discomfort that may be experienced by some patients.

Companies are also seeking to leverage advances in high-speed wireless communication to enable physician monitoring of the patient outside of traditional medical environments, for example, the patient's home. Schwartz sees the opportunity to develop a new class of medical products that could "even act as an object of beauty and curiosity in the home," much like the iMac brought computers out of the remote study and into the living room. The ultimate goal is to increase overall usage and improve treatment compliance and effectiveness by connecting to people's lifestyles.

In each of these cases, the technology by itself misses part of the product opportunity: the emotion-based part. Yet by themselves, new technologies like nanotechnology have emotional connotations, including the hope of the future and fear of the unknown. The goal is to leverage the positive emotional attributes of a technology into delivery of the overall product experience.

Nanotechnology and other new technologies will continue to spur the development of new medical products that will beneficially impact the lives of millions of people and provide new profit streams to companies. For successful product development and technology adoption, it will be critical to design new technology products to address function and simultaneously leverage the opportunities connected with satisfying patients' emotional needs and desires.

Emotion of Space Systems: Emotion Out of This World

Satellites, rocket ships, interplanetary robotic rovers: One doesn't normally associate emotion with the design of highly technical products such as aerospace systems, which people will not see or physically interact with once launched and in use. According to Erik Antonsson, Professor of Mechanical Engineering at Cal Tech and Director of Research for Northrop Grumman, emotion plays an important role in the technology's design.

On one hand, there is the pride that engineers feel in creating the technology, yet they know that the average person looking at their Rube Goldberg–appearing devices might not appreciate the elegance of the technology. Their inventions have to look elegant in order to be associated with elegance, to appear carefully designed so they can be credited with the sophistication equal to its technological capabilities.

On the other hand is the natural preference that people have for aesthetically pleasing designs. Antonsson says, "Symmetry appears to play an important role in our judgment of appearance. Not surprisingly then, unless there is an overriding reason not to do so, engineers create configurations of new devices and systems that are symmetric, even where no considerations of aesthetics play a role in the success."

Consider, for example, the configuration of the NASA Mars Exploration Rovers. These vehicles operate on a planet uninhabited by humans. Since it will be unseen after launch, one might expect the engineers to be completely unconcerned with its appearance. However, it turns out that many nontechnical observers of the

FIGURE 9.2 ■ U.S. Design Patent D487,715.

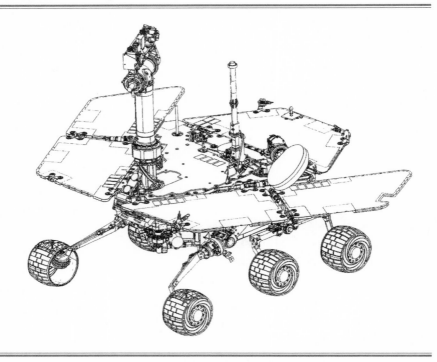

Rover's configuration respond positively to its appearance, so much so that NASA has patented their design through a design patent[35] (see Figure 9.2). Antonsson points out that one aspect of the design is perfect bilateral symmetry. Although useful for performance in unknown environmental conditions, the symmetric design also naturally resonates with people's emotions.

The appearance and visually pleasing configuration of technical devices and systems also plays an important role in what are typically called programmatic decisions: those decisions having to do with the selection of projects to fund. According to Antonsson, "In these decisions, the enumeration of technical performances of a proposed system are the formal basis for selection; however, proposers understand that programmatic decision makers will have a range of options to choose among, all with competing capabilities and performances. Here, proposers understand that one of the few aspects that can distinguish one proposed system from another is its visual appearance and pleasing configuration. Few decision makers wish to be seen to be choosing an unappealing or ugly system, if attractive options with nearly equal performance and capability are available. Perhaps these considerations should not be present in technical decisions, yet the visual appearance connects to the decision maker's emotions, such as security, confidence and pride, and their natural sense of balance."

Engineering designs are not solely judged by their technical attributes, nor can they be reduced to an unemotional list of performances that are evaluated in purely numerical terms. Engineering designs appeal directly to our emotions; they are expressive and they are persuasive. Even in highly technical environments where humans will not function or see the devices, such as unmanned missions in space, core emotional desires turn out to be relevant factors of success.

The Role of Emotion in Robotics: Your Friend, the Robot

Given that other technologies have product emotions, it will not be terribly surprising that robots are similarly capable of evoking emotions. After all, robots in the movies are almost human, for example WALL·E, that adorable and caring robot animated by Pixar. However, looking at real-world robots instead of movie-star robots, the idea of emotional robots may seem unusual.

Robots today are increasingly commonplace, not serving as friend and comrade in an adventure but laboring alone in dull, routine activities in the world of manufacturing or exploring hard-to-reach places. These mechanistic robots, which rarely look even remotely human, find value in places that are dangerous, dirty, and dull, creating the opportunity for companies such as RedZone Robotics (discussed in Chapter 6).

Robots are typically thought of as aids in a physical world, but the potential for robots to assist in social and emotion-related ways in a variety of human activities is also great, revealing new emotion-based opportunities for today's technology.

One such area that is experiencing rapid growth is *socially assistive robotics* (SAR). SAR is a new field that focuses on developing robots capable of assisting users through *social* rather than *physical* interaction. The robot's physical embodiment is at the heart of SAR's assistive effectiveness, as it leverages the inherently human tendency to engage with lifelike (but not necessarily human-like or animal-like) social behavior.

Maja Matarić is a Professor of Computer Science and Neuroscience at the University of Southern California and a pioneer in the field of SAR. Matarić notes that people, it turns out, readily ascribe intention, personality, and emotion to even the simplest robots, from LEGO toys to iRobot Roomba vacuum cleaners.

SAR uses this human-robot connection to develop socially interactive robots capable of monitoring, motivating, encouraging, and sustaining user activities and improving human performance. SAR has the potential to enhance the quality of life for large populations of users, including the elderly, individuals with cognitive impairments, those rehabilitating from stroke and other neuromotor disabilities, and children with sociodevelopmental disorders such as autism.

Robots can help improve the function of a wide variety of people, not just functionally but also socially, by embracing and augmenting the emotional connection between human and robot. To do so, an effective socially assistive robot must understand and interact with its environment, exhibit social behavior, focus its attention and communication on the user, sustain engagement with the user, and achieve specific assistive goals. The robot must do all of this through social rather than physical interaction, and it must do all of this in a way that is safe, ethical, and effective for the potentially vulnerable user.

As with WALL•E, according to Matarić, in SAR, *believability* plays a more important role than realism. Matarić and her team found that anthropomorphic yet not highly realistic appearance is well suited to assistive tasks. At the same time, key issues such as keeping robot size smaller than the user, and the robot being sufficiently light and weak to minimize any physical risk must be maintained.

Matarić says, "The robot's personality, expressed through embodied and verbal interaction, is likely more important than its physical appearance, and verbal interactions are more important than the robot's physical expression."[36,37] Further, "The physical look and presence of the robot appears to play a key role in its perceived social engagement and empathy, with users reporting being more 'cared for' and 'watched over' by physically embodied robots as opposed to computer software agents."[38]

Social engagement that builds on physical interaction between robot and user can begin to ascribe personality to the robot, even during short interactions. When the robot's personality (expressed through the amount of movement and the volume, pitch, and content of speech) is matched with the user's demeanor (obtained through a standard personality test), users perform longer and better on a task. Based on galvanic skin response,[39] Matarić could predict when a user was about to quit a task.[40]

Matarić's robots are able to measure certain unexpressed emotions. A robot with access to such unexpressed emotional cues about the user can appropri-

FIGURE 9.3 ■ Socially assistive robots from the Interaction Lab, University of Southern California: a platform, one interacting with a child with autism spectrum disorder, and one interacting with an elderly user.

Photos by permission from Maja J. Matarić

ately adjust its own emotional response (through tone of voice, content of speech, facial expressions, body pose, or personal distance) to continue to motivate the user appropriately.

Matarić says, "Much remains to be learned about personality and its expression through emotional and other factors in the context of human-machine interaction, but the potential is great." She creates robots that sustain interaction with stroke patients, children with autism, and the elderly population, especially those suffering from cognitive loss through dementia and Alzheimer's disease (see Figure 9.3).

Emotion-based technology is real.

Emotion of Technology

Technology evokes emotions in its users, whether in consumer or business-to-business markets. It is not simply reactions to the new: optimism about future capabilities or pessimism about what may go wrong. Technology can fulfill emotion-based opportunities.

Patients primarily want to get well but they also value an experience that is more than coldly clinical. People want to see the technology they use, but they appreciate passion in its impact when they don't. Buyers of space systems primarily seek functional capabilities but they appreciate the pleasure of aesthetics and clean design. Real-world robots have typically worked in place of humans but their ability to interact with humans allows them to address emotions, such as inspiring hope as they patiently encourage rehabilitation patients. Even raw technology can be designed to engender product emotions valued in the marketplace.

The diversity of examples in Chapters 8 and 9 illustrate that emotion is relevant practically everywhere, providing proven value and purchase motivation in both consumer and business-to-business markets. What remains is to bring all the ideas in *Built to Love* together and guide you to implement them within your company.

For that, we turn to the final chapter.

CHAPTER 10

Taking Action:
Transform Your Products and Brands to Captivate Customers

Emotion must be embraced in the most in-touch consumer company as well as the most mundane B-to-B company, for emotion is human and its reach is vast. The examples in the past two chapters examine the extremes, ranging from societal issues capturing a deep emotional belief to raw technology that, on first thought, would be far removed from emotion.

Whether the product is a technology, a program to address a social issue, or anything else designed to be purchased by and used by humans, there is an emotion-based business opportunity to be discovered. From customer to employee, from social service to emerging technology, customers and other users have core desires and hopes that can only be fulfilled emotionally.

Built to Love has introduced new evidence of the power of emotion in business along with a means to rigorously identify, assess, and design for emotions that customers seek in the products that they buy and use, whether those products are physical products, services, systems, software products, or brands.

The final step is to summarize and bring together the detailed approaches in this book, providing a vision for creating new products that fulfill the emotions of the user. The Model of Creating Products that Captivate Customers, shown again in Figure 10.1, will guide you back to the fundamental ideas of *Built to Love* and provide a process to move from emotion-based opportunities to product solutions.

Any business opportunity begins with human needs, and *Built to Love* shows that emotions must be fulfilled. The process therefore begins with determining which product emotion categories people in your target market look to fulfill with your products. Then, using the eMap, you must craft a specific emotion strategy from which to design a product. For example, among other attributes, the emotion strategy of Publicolor includes *hope*, and the emotion strategy of socially assistive robots (SAR) includes *encouragement*.

FIGURE 10.1 ◼ Model of Creating Products that Captivate Customers: How to create products built to love.

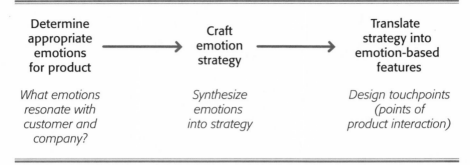

The final step is to translate the product strategy into one or more prodcts through touchpoints, designed to stimulate the product emotions that comprise the product emotion strategy. For Publicolor, one touchpoint was as simple as the walls of the school, a starting point for many more interactions. For SAR, researchers found that verbal interaction of robots was a more effective touchpoint than visual appearance, indicating where they should put a greater share of their efforts and resources.

Now that you've read *Built to Love*, the Model of Creating Products that Captivate Customers is quite simple: Investigate and analyze what emotions should be evoked, build that capability into the product, then let the product perform. That's what happened with Publicolor and SAR. That's what happened with all the other examples, such as Trash Talk, which delivered emotions of passion, pride, and compassion—categories relevant to sustainability—in a visible patchwork, bright colors, and unique sole of the final product, sneakers made from otherwise wasted materials (as seen in Figure 8.1 in Chapter 8).

Move Ahead: Fast or Slow

Have you ever tried to go swimming in the ocean in northern Maine? It's a tough thing to do. Experience will tell you that once you are in the water you will be comfortable; those already in the water are telling you this. You either trust them and plunge in, dealing with the shock of change but enjoying yourself once you adapt to the temperature, or you take your time, slowly putting your toes in, then your legs, your upper body, and then your head.

You may take either approach to incorporating emotion into your product. You can trust the experiences of others and dive right in, or take your time and slowly immerse yourself. There are potential risks and benefits to both approaches. Either approach is fine, as long as you choose one.

The Plunge

To take the plunge, start with a critical assessment of your portfolio of products. Your portfolio may exist within a brand, sub-brand, division, or product group. Use the eMap to assess your firm's current state and your competitors' state. Your firm's current state is the set of emotions that your product portfolio already delivers to your customers. Your competitors' state is the set of emotions that their products deliver to their customers. This assessment should reflect the customers' perspective, and should be derived from research on customers about how they perceive current products.

In addition to researching your customers' perception of current product offerings, you should also determine how they would want to perceive future products, a market research task that admittedly requires some care. Knowing what they desire will help you define what your product portfolio will deliver and what your portfolio should become in terms of what emotions it delivers to customers.

This is the basis for your product emotion strategy. Importantly, the emotion strategy for your product portfolio must include what your customers seek, but it is not entirely defined by your customers' needs. Your emotion strategy also must incorporate that which is unique about your firm, your company's capabilities, and how it is differentiated in the market. Again, the eMap will help you identify which emotions are strongest and what attributes define the emotions of your product portfolio.

Based on the eMap analysis and the resulting identified attributes, you can craft your emotion strategy for your product portfolio. Seek to organize the attributes as a concise statement or as a dimensional continuum, possibly from core or foundational to some attribute such as provocative, powerful, playful, or other.

Often, the product emotion strategy is an internal statement that drives all strategy relevant to the set of products within that portfolio, be it the products of a firm, division, or brand. Any products that you develop should fit within the emotion strategy. However, products will also have individual attributes and identities that should be complementary to the overall emotion strategy for that brand or family of products. Navistar's International LoneStar and ProStar both were de-rived from the Integrated Brand Identity map of Figure 7.9, and both fit within the "challenges convention" mantra. Yet LoneStar targeted the higher-end market with a provocative product, while ProStar targeted the mainstream, workhorse market. They worked in concert to establish the identity of that product portfolio—the brand identity of Navistar's truck division.

Slow and Steady

The alternative to the plunge—the slow-and-steady approach—will start with the development of a single product. This might be one that is new or a revision of an existing product that needs to be refreshed. Possibly the product under re-vision is the market leader but is vulnerable to the competition. Or possibly you have a product that is currently number two or three, but there is opportunity to eat into number one's market share, or even take over the leader position. You know that you need to do something different, and here is your chance to dip your toe into designing product emotions.

You may do something as simple as identifying one or two new touchpoints that will resonate emotionally with your potential customers, enough to see the impact without abandoning the current course. Of course, the less you do, the fewer commitments you make to an overall, emotion-based design, the less im-pact you will see. Quite possibly, if you are too conservative in your risk, you may end up seeing no real effect from the changes.

Regardless of the outcome, your first effort or two will give you experience. This initial effort sets you up to expand your emotion-based product develop-ment endeavors. Over time you will see the impact of your emerging strategy. At that point you should formalize your emotion-based brand strategy for your overall product portfolio.

Your process should use the eMap, based on research of the needs and wants of your customer base. You may need to begin using ethnographic methods of observation and qualitative surveys to uncover those needs and wants. The eMap will inform you as to which attributes resonate deepest with your customers (and potential customers). Your development team must then envision which touchpoints can be used to fulfill those attributes.

Once you are ready to redefine or formalize your emotion-based brand strat-egy, the eMap is used at the overall portfolio level to understand which emotions will exude from your set of potential products.

Tradeoffs

The plunge approach has the benefit of improving your product and brand stature and margins quickly. The difficulty is in making sure that the majority of your employees are on board. The slow-and-steady tactic has the benefit of initial results, proving to others in the company that emotion will pay off and, slowly, getting others to buy in. At the same time, your competitor may successfully take the plunge and then you will be stuck playing catch up, once again.

Determine which of the two approaches is comfortable for you and how confident you are in your ability to embrace emotion. You may want to begin with a test case or two. Maybe identify a negative emotion and transform it to a positive one. Then, with confidence and experience, take the plunge in everything you do henceforth as a company.

Either way, it's your turn to look around at all the emotion-based opportunities in the world. You decide which to fulfill, and consider how to address them. It's your turn to use the Model of Creating Products that Captivate Customers to build products that people love. You can engage and captivate your customers by authentically fulfilling not just their functional needs but also their emotional needs and desires with your products, services, and brands. You can make a difference in their lives.

In turn, your customers will reward you by spending their resources to increase your profits, short-term and long-term. *Built to Love* has provided you with a vision and proof that the task is worth your effort.

Embrace the change.

Now it is up to you to act on this foundation and create the next high-emotion product, or better yet, the next high-emotion index company.

Acknowledgments

As with any good product, many people have helped in developing this book. Several in particular we wish to thank.

A variety of prominent people gave us their time to develop the case studies found in the book. We especially thank Jared Cohon, President, and Bonnie Cersosimo, Associate VP of Marketing and Media Relations, at Carnegie Mellon University; Craig Vogel, Professor of Design and founder of the Live Well Collaborative at the University of Cincinnati; William Mitchell, Alexander Dreyfoos Professor of Architecture and Media Arts and Sciences at MIT, Director of the Smart Cities group at the MIT Media Lab, and Director of the MIT Design Laboratory; Maja Matarić, Professor of Computer Science, Neuroscience, and Pediatrics, and founding Director of the Center for Robotics and Embedded Systems at the University of Southern California; Xiangyang Xin, Assistant Professor of Design and Program Leader of the Master of Design at the Hong Kong Polytechnic University; Philip LeDuc, Associate Professor of Mechanical Engineering at Carnegie Mellon University with appointments in Biomedical Engineering and Biological Sciences; Erik Antonsson, Director of Research for the Northrop Grumman Aerospace Systems Corporation, and Professor of Mechanical Engineering at Cal Tech; Robert Schwartz, General Manager of Global Design for GE Health Care; Ruth Lande Shuman, founder and President of Publicolor; and Kasey Jarvis, Industrial Designer and Innovator at Nike.

We have also been fortunate to work with outstanding leaders in product development who helped to develop several other case studies throughout the book. We are grateful to the collaboration and assistance from Dee Kapur (President), Dave Allendorph (Chief Designer), and Al Saltiel (VP of Marketing) at Navistar International Truck; Eric Close, President of RedZone Robotics; Ed Pupa (President and CEO) and Tony Ryan (Chief Technology Officer) at

DesignAdvance Systems; Craig Shein, Managing Director at Dormont Manufacturing; and Chuck Jones (VP of Global Brands) and Kevin Gilboe (Senior Brand Manager) at Whirlpool.

We are fortunate to teach at a first-rate university with some of the best students in the world. Several have worked with us on research projects that provided the basis for research presented in this book. We appreciate the assistance of Joshua Chaise, Tanuka Ghoshal, Seth Orsborn, Melissa Appel Nahmias, Adina Klein, Gaku Sato, Tiffany Yang, Jay McCormack, and Michael Pugliese. We also appreciate Caryn Audenried, Alexandra Garrity, and Ying (Linda) Lee's assistance in creating the figures in the book. Thanks also to Melissa Cagan and Andrew Cagan for their photographic assistance.

We are particularly thankful to have Berrett-Koehler as our publisher. Working with Berrett-Koehler has been a unique and rewarding experience with their level of effort and enthusiasm in refining the book. We enjoyed working with President and Publisher Steve Piersanti and Executive Managing Editor Jeevan Siva while bringing this book to production, and we are appreciative of their suggestions to improve the book. We appreciate the guidance of our agent, Susan Schulman, for her support and advice through the writing process. We are also appreciative of suggestions from Jenny Williams, Travis Wilson, Dave Wood, and Josh O'Conner. We would like to thank Ken Jennings for introducing us to Berrett-Koehler.

Finally, it is a privilege to be on the faculty of Carnegie Mellon. The faculty, staff, and students at Carnegie Mellon are some of the best in the world, and many have directly or indirectly influenced the ideas of this book.

NOTE FROM THE AUTHORS: As *Built to Love* was going to press, Prof. William Mitchell, who contributed to our discussion of emotion and buildings in Chapter 7, passed away. Bill was a good friend and mentor, and we will miss him.

Notes

Chapter 1

1. Lerner, J. S., D. A. Small, and G. Loewenstein (2004) "Heart Strings and Purse Strings." *Psychological Science*, Vol. 15, No. 5 (Aug) pp. 337–341.

2. Zhu, R., and J. Meyers-Levy (2005) *Journal of Marketing Research*, Vol. XLII (August), pp. 333–345.

3. "How Google Fuels Its Idea Factory," *Business Week*, May 12, 2008, p. 54.

Chapter 2

4. "The Black & Decker Corporation (A): Power Tools Division," Harvard Business School Case #9-595-057, Harvard Business School Publishing, 1995, p. 1.

5. "The Black & Decker Corporation (A): Power Tools Division," Harvard Business School Case #9-595-057, Harvard Business School Publishing, 1995, p. 9.

6. "Black & Decker Corporation Series," Harvard Business School Case #5-598-106, Harvard Business School Publishing, 1998, p. 1.

7. Schorn, D., "Howard Schultz: The Star of Starbucks," 4/23/2006, available at www.cbsnews.com/stories/2006/04/21/60minutes/main1532246.shtml.

Chapter 4

8. *The Oxford Dictionary of English* (2nd edition revised).

9. Our study follows up on Carpenter, G. S., R. Glazer, and K. Nakamoto (1994) "Meaningful Brands from Meaningless Differentiation: The Dependence of Irrelevant Attributes," *Journal of Marketing Research*, Vol. 31, No. 3 (Aug) pp. 339–350, which had noted the value difference in "Alpine" and "regular" but had not investigated the emotional value evoked by these words.

10. Again, this study builds on Carpenter, G. S., R. Glazer, and K. Nakamoto (1994).

11. Plassmann, H., J. O'Doherty, B. Shiv, and A. Rangel (2008) "Marketing Actions Can Modulate Neural Representations of Experienced Pleasantness," Proceedings of the National Academy of Sciences, Vol. 105, No. 3, pp. 1050–1054.

12. Stuettgen, P., J. Vosgerau, P. Boatwright, and C. Messner (2009) "Adding Significance to the Implicit Association Test," Working paper, Carnegie Mellon University.

Chapter 5

13. www.qwertyrash.com/archives/apple-iworks-numbers-the-new-killer-app/

14. Ghoshal, T., P. Boatwright and J. Cagan (2010) "Unwrapping Packaging: Does It Pay, and 'How'!—The Role of Aesthetically Appealing Packaging in Product Valuation," Working paper, Carnegie Mellon University.

15. "BMW Introduces Joy to Its Olympic Marketing Efforts," PR Newswire, Feb 13, 2010.

Chapter 6

16. Osgood, C. E., Suci, G. J., and Tannenbaum, P. H. (1957) The Measurement of Meaning, Urbana: University of Illinois Press.

17. See Chapter 7 of Cagan, J., and C. Vogel (2001) Creating Breakthrough Products: Innovation from Product Planning to Program Approval, Upper Saddle River, NJ: Financial Times Prentice Hall, for examples of ethnography in practice, or see the wine study discussed in Chapter 4 for an example of the use of both fMRI and self-explicated surveys, two different methods that yielded the same information.

18. Norman, D. A. (2004) Emotional Design, New York: Basic Books.

Chapter 7

19. Pugliese, M. and J. Cagan (2002) "Capturing a Rebel: Modeling the Harley-Davidson Brand through a Motorcycle Shape Grammar," Research in Engineering Design, Vol. 13, no. 3, pp. 139–156.

20. Ibid.

21. From McCormack, J. P., J. Cagan, and C. M. Vogel (2004) "Speaking the Buick Language: Capturing, Understanding, and Exploring Brand Identity with Shape Grammars," Design Studies, Vol. 25, pp. 1–29.

22. Durr, K., and L. Sullivan (2007), International Harvester, McCormack, International—Milestones in the Company that Helped Build America, Graphic Arts Center Publishing Company, pp. 210–215.

23. From Boatwright, P., J. Cagan, D. Kapur, and A. Saltiel (2009) "A Step-by-Step Process to Build Valued Brands," *Journal of Product and Brand Management*, Vol. 18, no. 1, pp. 38–49.

24. Cagan, J., and C. M. Vogel (2002) *Creating Breakthrough Products: Innovation from Product Planning to Program Approval*, Upper Saddle River, NJ: Financial Times Prentice Hall.

25. www.caranddriver.com/reviews/car/00q4/pontiac_aztek_gt-road_test

26. For the details of these shape grammars and a demonstration of their power in design see: Pugliese, M., and J. Cagan (2002) "Capturing a Rebel: Modeling the Harley-Davidson Brand through a Motorcycle Shape Grammar," *Research in Engineering Design*, Vol. 13, no. 3, pp. 139–156; and McCormack, J. P., J. Cagan, and C. M. Vogel (2004) "Speaking the Buick Language: Capturing, Understanding, and Exploring Brand Identity with Shape Grammars," *Design Studies*, Vol. 25, pp. 1–29.

27. A nice discussion of shape computation and shape grammars is found in Stiny, G. (2006) *Shape*, Cambridge, MA: MIT Press.

28. For details see Orsborn, S., J. Cagan, and P. Boatwright (2009) "Quantifying Aesthetic Form Preference in a Utility Function," *ASME Journal of Mechanical Design*, Vol. 131, 061001-1-10; and Orsborn, S., and J. Cagan (2009) "Automatically Generating Form Concepts According to Consumer Preference: A Shape Grammar Implementation with Software Agents," *ASME Journal of Mechanical Design*, Vol. 131, 121007-1-10.

29. *Dictionary of Philosophy and Psychology* (1957), edited by James Mark Baldwin, Gloucester, MA: Peter Smith Publishing.

30. For details, see note 28.

31. *The Encyclopedia of Philosophy* (1967) edited by Paul Edwards. New York: MacMillan, p. 36.

Chapter 8

32. Xin, X., J. Cagan, and C. Vogel (August 28–31, 2007) "Interpreting Cultural Artifacts," *ICED 07*, International Conference on Engineering Design, Paris.

33. Xiangyang, X. (2007) *Product Innovation in a Cultural Context: A Method Applied to Chinese Product Development*, PhD dissertation, Carnegie Mellon University, Pittsburgh, PA.

Chapter 9

34. LeDuc, P., M. Wong, et al. (2007). "Toward an *In Vivo* Biologically Inspired Nanofactory," *Nature Nanotechnology*, Vol. 2, pp. 3–7.

35. In the U.S. Patent and Trademark Office, a design patent, as distinguished from a utility patent, protects the way a device or system appears, as opposed to functions.

36. Matarić, M. J., J. Eriksson, D. Feil-Seifer, and C. Winstein (Feb 19, 2007) "Socially Assistive Robotics for Post-Stroke Rehabilitation," *International Journal of NeuroEngineering and Rehabilitation*, Vol. 4, No. 5.

37. Mower, E. K., S. Lee, M. J. Matarić, and S. Narayanan (Mar 30–Apr 4, 2008) "Human Perception of Synthetic Character Emotions in the Presence of Conflicting and Congruent Vocal and Facial Expressions," *Proceedings of the International Conference on Acoustics, Speech, and Signal Processing (ICASSP-08)*, Las Vegas, NV.

38. Wainer, J., D. J. Feil-Seifer, D. Shell, and M. J. Matarić (Sep 6–8, 2006) "The Role of Physical Embodiment in Human-Robot Interaction," *Proceedings of the 15th International Workshop on Robot and Human Interactive Communication (RO-MAN 2006)*, U. of Hertfordshire, Hatfield, UK.

39. Tapus, A., C. Tapus, and M. J. Matarić (2008) "User-Robot Personality Matching and Assistive Robot Behavior Adaptation for Post-Stroke Rehabilitation Therapy," *Intelligent Service Robotics Journal*, Special Issue on Multidisciplinary Collaboration for Socially Assistive Robotics, A. Tapus, ed.

40. Mower, E. K., D. J. Feil-Seifer, M. J Matarić, and S. Narayanan (2007) "Investigating Implicit Cues for User State Estimation in Human-Robot Interaction Using Physiological Measurements, *Proceedings of the 16th International Workshop on Robot and Human Interactive Communication (RO-MAN 2007)*, Jeju Island, South Korea.

Index

About the Authors

Photo by www.harrygiglio.com

Globally known for their rigorous and effective approach to product innovation, Professors Peter Boatwright and Jonathan Cagan collaborate in corporate consulting, research on innovation processes and tools, teaching and leading innovation teams, and speaking engagements on the topic of innovation.

Peter Boatwright (foreground) is an Associate Professor of Marketing at the Tepper School of Business.

Jonathan Cagan is the George Tallman and Florence Barrett Ladd Professor in the Department of Mechanical Engineering at Carnegie Mellon University.

In the Carnegie Mellon tradition, Boatwright also has an appointment in the Department of Mechanical Engineering, and Cagan in the Schools of Design and Computer Science.

Boatwright and Cagan actively consult with companies ranging from Fortune 100 to entrepreneurial startups, with a focus on product strategy and innovation as well as brand strategy. They have applied their formal approaches to opportunity identification and product development in their work with a diverse range of companies, including International Truck/Navistar, Apple, P&G, Dormont Manufacturing, Bayer MaterialScience, Respironics, MSA, Whirlpool, Lubrizol, Kennametal, Alcoa, RedZone Robotics, DesignAdvance Systems, Industrial Scientific, New Balance, and Giant Eagle, among others.

Boatwright and Cagan co-lead executive training sessions. They also co-teach practice-based courses at the university, including an annual course on new product innovation and other product strategy courses, resulting in multiple patents for corporate sponsors. They also actively collaborate on research in innovation methods and have co-authored a previous book, *The Design of Things to Come: How Ordinary People Create Extraordinary Products*. Between their consulting, corporate projects, and innovation courses they have advised over 200 product innovation teams.

Professor Boatwright's expertise and teaching focuses on innovation, new product marketing and brand strategy, and marketing research methods. Through research, Boatwright has developed new statistical methods as well as additional theories of consumer behavior, spanning qualitative and quantitative methodologies, studying consumer response, product assortment, and early product research methods. Dr. Boatwright has an MS in Statistics from University of Wisconsin, and his MBA and PhD are from University of Chicago's Booth School of Business. Boatwright's scholarly articles appear in leading research journals in the fields of marketing, statistics, and management.

Professor Cagan is an expert in product development and innovation methods for early-stage product development, computational design, and cognitive mechanisms for innovation. Both his design methods and computer-based design research have been applied in a variety of industries. He co-founded and served as Chief Technologist of DesignAdvance Systems, Inc., a company focused on developing CAD software for the early synthesis processes. Cagan has authored over 150 publications. He is the co-author of a third book, *Creating Breakthrough Products: Innovation from Product Planning to Program Approval*. He co-founded and co-directs the Master of Product Development program at Carnegie Mellon. Cagan has several issued and pending patents, is a licensed Professional Engineer, and is a Fellow of the American Society of Mechanical Engineers. Cagan received his PhD from University of California at Berkeley after working for the Eastman Kodak Company. He has been on the faculty of Carnegie Mellon since 1990.

Learn More

For more information about *Built to Love*, or to contact the authors about speaking engagements, visit: www.BuiltToLove.com.

For information on Boatwright and Cagan's consulting, visit:
www.CarnegieStrategies.com.

For information on Professor Boatwright's academic research and teaching, visit:
www.tepper.cmu.edu/facultydirectory.

For information on Professor Cagan's academic research and teaching, visit:
www.cmu.edu/me/people/jonathan-cagan.html.

Berrett–Koehler
Publishers

Berrett-Koehler is an independent publisher dedicated to an ambitious mission: *Creating a World That Works for All*.

We believe that to truly create a better world, action is needed at all levels— individual, organizational, and societal. At the individual level, our publications help people align their lives with their values and with their aspirations for a better world. At the organizational level, our publications promote progressive leadership and management practices, socially responsible approaches to business, and humane and effective organizations. At the societal level, our publications advance social and economic justice, shared prosperity, sustainability, and new solutions to national and global issues.

A major theme of our publications is "Opening Up New Space." Berrett-Koehler titles challenge conventional thinking, introduce new ideas, and foster positive change. Their common quest is changing the underlying beliefs, mindsets, institutions, and structures that keep generating the same cycles of problems, no matter who our leaders are or what improvement programs we adopt.

We strive to practice what we preach—to operate our publishing company in line with the ideas in our books. At the core of our approach is stewardship, which we define as a deep sense of responsibility to administer the company for the benefit of all of our "stakeholder" groups: authors, customers, employees, investors, service providers, and the communities and environment around us.

We are grateful to the thousands of readers, authors, and other friends of the company who consider themselves to be part of the "BK Community." We hope that you, too, will join us in our mission.

A BK Business Book

This book is part of our BK Business series. BK Business titles pioneer new and progressive leadership and management practices in all types of public, private, and nonprofit organizations. They promote socially responsible approaches to business, innovative organizational change methods, and more humane and effective organizations.

Berrett–Koehler
Publishers

A community dedicated to creating
a world that works for all

Visit Our Website: www.bkconnection.com

Read book excerpts, see author videos and Internet movies, read our authors' blogs, join discussion groups, download book apps, find out about the BK Affiliate Network, browse subject-area libraries of books, get special discounts, and more!

Subscribe to Our Free E-Newsletter, the *BK Communiqué*

Be the first to hear about new publications, special discount offers, exclusive articles, news about bestsellers, and more! Get on the list for our free e-newsletter by going to **www.bkconnection.com**.

Get Quantity Discounts

Berrett-Koehler books are available at quantity discounts for orders of ten or more copies. Please call us toll-free at (800) 929-2929 or email us at **bkp .orders@aidcvt.com**.

Join the BK Community

BKcommunity.com is a virtual meeting place where people from around the world can engage with kindred spirits to create a world that works for all. BKcommunity.com members may create their own profiles, blog, start and participate in forums and discussion groups, post photos and videos, answer surveys, announce and register for upcoming events, and chat with others online in real time. Please join the conversation!